Pendle

&

its Surroundings

by
Dr. Spencer T. Hall

Illustrations by
Wm. Angelo Waddington

Foreword by
Roger Frost

Landy Publishing
1995

'Pendle Hill & its Surroundings' was first published in 1877.
Copyright on this 1995 edition is held by Landy Publishing
and by Roger Frost.

The cover photograph of Pendle Hill is by
Foxley Photography, Church Street, Colne.

ISBN. 1. 872895 . 24 . 7.

Landy Publishing have also published:-

Lancashire Limericks. by John Sephton.
In Fine Fettle. dialect poems by Peter Thornley & Michael May.
Annals of Trawden Forest. by Fred Bannister.
In Lancashire Language. dialect poems edited by Bob Dobson
Accrington Observed. by Brian Brindle & Bob Dobson.
A Blackburn Miscellany. edited by Bob Dobson.
A full list of publications is available from;

Landy Publishing.
3 Staining Rise
Staining
Blackpool FY3 0BU.
Tel. / Fax. 01253 886103.

(Postage is free on books despatched to U.K. customers.)

Printed & Produced in England
B.P.S. 01282 612983

Introduction

Spencer Timothy Hall was not a local man but, in his *"Pendle Hill and its Surroundings"* , he produced a charmingly typical mid-Victorian guide to an area of Lancashire in transition.

Though it lacks the detailed directions of more recent guides, the booklet can still be followed by the walker who will, even today over a hundred years later, be able to recognise and experience much of what the author recorded in the 1870's

Spencer T. Hall was born in 1812 at Brookside Cottage, Sutton-in-Ashfield, Nottinghamshire. The village was in the heart of Robin Hood country and from this, together with his father's nick name *(The Sherwood Forest Patriarch)*, he took the name by which he was better known, *"The Sherwood Forester"*

He was born into a humble home - Samuel, his father was a cobbler and his mother, Eleanor Spencer, a shepherdess. As a young boy, Spencer worked in the stocking-making industry, firstly as a winder, then a weaver.

It is clear that Spencer was an avid reader and upon reading a life of Benjamin Franklin he resolved to become a printer. This necessitated a move to Nottingham where, in 1829 , he was appprenticed as a printer to the *"Nottingham Mercury"*. Soon he had drawn attention to himself as a poet and he became involved in setting up a scientific institution in the town, at which he read several papers.

Contributions to many periodicals kept his name before the public but in 1836 he returned to Sutton-in-Ashfield where he set up in business as a printer and bookseller printing a monthly, the *"Sherwood Magazine"*.

In 1839 he moved to Yorkshire, but he never lost interest in the East Midlands . While in exile he produced *"The Forester's Offering"*, a volume of prose and poetry descriptive of the Sutton area, and throughout his life he continued, in his writings, to refer to his native area.

This can be seen in *"Pendle Hill and its Surroundings"*. It is dedicated to a lady from Nottinghamshire. When describing "Narrow-Yates" (now known as Narrowgates) near Barley, he compares it with Edale in Derbyshire. Higham, near Pendle, is mentioned in the same breath as the village of the same name, also in Derbyshire.

In Yorkshire he lived in both York and Sheffield and, in these years, he became interested in and lectured on phrenology and mesmerism. In these quasi-medical fields he became quite well known and even effected a cure on Harriet Martineau, the writer, when she appeared to be incurably ill.

Next we find him in Ireland at the time of the Famine and, in 1850, he published what can be regarded as his most important work, *"Life and Death in Ireland"*. This showed Hall to have a social conscience and again, we can see this in his *"Pendle Hill"*, especially when he refers to the newly - built *"Primrose Bank"*, the Burnley Union's institution.

For the rest of his life he practised in the field of homoeopathy in Kendal, Windermere, Burnley and on the Fylde coast. His last few years were spent in poverty, though he did receive a grant from the government. He died at Blackpool in 1885.

Spencer T. Hall's time in Burnley covers the 1870's. He lived and had consulting rooms at 102 Manchester Road in the town.

It is clear, from his writings, that he came to love our area of Lancashire and he became friends with people of like-mind-poets, naturalists and writers of whom he found many in the Burnley area.

Hall became involved in many petty and rather academic arguments and one feels that one of the motivations for his writings was a degree of self justification. However, that should not detract from much of the content of his books.

Particularly admirable are his brief pen-sketches of the places he visits. For example, he describes Pendle Hill as *"...wooer of winds and parent of streams"*, and Pendle Water he refers to as *"..rushing and gurgling, now flowing less rapidly, and whispering sermons in the stones"*. I am very fond of what Hall says of Haggate, a village in my native Briercliffe. He calls it *"...far-seen and far seeing Haggate "* and *"...chapel- crowned Haggate"*. When you take his advice and walk in the area you will see how accurate, even today, are his descriptions.

Consider his few words *"...the little Manchester of the Forest"*, which he ascribes to Barrowford and how apposite they were in 1877.

There are numerous extracts I could quote but particularly good are his descriptions of Burnley and of an old man he meets in Nelson. This latter is worth a few words. *"...This last, bent, stiff-kneed vestige of the ancient population, in his old round hat, corduroy brecks, smock-frock and*

*greasy fustian gaiters, a short pipe in his mouth, and a spade...over his
shoulder... "*
In conclusion, I hope you enjoy following Spencer T. Hall as he gently
guides you around the district dominated by Pendle.

I have included the original illustrations together with a few more from
the Burnley architect William Angelo Waddington. These are taken from
Waddington's *" Sketches on the Calder and the Ribble in and around
Whalley "* and were executed when the artist was a precocious young man,
not long before Hall came to Burnley.

Hall mentions W.A. Waddington in *"Pendle Hill... "* so it is not out of
place that these illustrations have been added. One feels that Hall would
have approved.

Roger Frost,
Briercliffe, 1995.

DEDICATION.

——:o:——

To MRS. CHAWORTH-MUSTERS,

Annesley Park and Wiverton, Notts.

DEAR MADAM,

As one of the most gifted and respected gentle-women in my native district, will you favour me with permission to inscribe to you this little Handbook, written in the spirit of other works of which you have sometimes honoured and gladdened me by expressing a generous approbation?

When in an occasional hour of leisure I have been able to mate with nature amid some of the scenes herein described, many things have so reminded me of dear old Sherwood Forest, and of well known attractions both in Nottinghamshire and Derbyshire around it, as to make me for the moment almost forget I was not there. All old English domains have necessarily something in common; and Annesley, with its surroundings, has many features akin to those of which several in these more northern regions have a right to boast.

Whilst you, and the family so dear to you, are enjoying those—celebrated as they are, not only for their natural beauty but in history and song; I shall possibly feel more than before at home in these, if hereafter associating with them, though only in print, your ever honoured name,—remaining,

Dear Madam,

Your obliged and most respectful

Friend and Servant,

THE AUTHOR.

PENDLE HILL

AND

ITS SURROUNDINGS;

INCLUDING

BURNLEY AND ITS BOUNDARIES:

BY

DR. SPENCER T. HALL, M.A.,

AUTHOR OF

"The Forester's Offering," "Rambles in the Country," "The Peak and the Plain," "Days in Derbyshire," "Biographical Sketches of Remarkable People," &c.

"We thank Thee, O God, for the mountains!"—
Mary Howitt.

LONDON:

SIMPKIN, MARSHALL, AND CO.

ROCHDALE: E. WRIGLEY AND SONS, PRINTERS.

MDCCCLXXVII.

PENDLE HILL.

PREFACE.

—o—

THIS free-hand *brochure* makes no pretension to the office of a gazetteer, but touches more on some of the ancient and natural aspects of a large and important district than on its civic institutions and ever-changing commercial and social features, though some of these may not have been altogether overlooked.

A person of great distinction and acknowledged taste and learning, having done me the honour to read my poem of "Pendle Hill" herein embodied, afterwards intimated how much he liked it, but that, though acquainted with the outlines of scenes to which it referred, he was less so with their filling up and history. On my mention of this to Mr. Alfred Strange, he at once said, "then why not write out some of the more interesting details wanted?" The idea took root; and from it what is here presented has grown.

With this plain introduction, what I have written is now issued. Probably none more than myself will be struck by its defects, including many omissions. But I trust these will be compensated for by what, if good nature accepts it, criticism may not despise.

In justice to my own feelings, I could not allow the little work to appear without expressing my obligations to Mr. Strange and several other neighbours and friends, who have aided me with books of reference or with kindly personal suggestions; also Mr. G. Toulmin, of the *Preston Guardian*, for favouring me with reflexes of the woodcuts of Towneley and Gawthorpe Halls; and should its perusal afford half as much enjoyment to the reader as its production has done to me, it will not have been written in vain.

Though so far from the scenes that gave me birth and (through my then young friend, Mr. Geo. B. Dalby,) my early literary *sobriquet*, let me once more, in affectionate memory of them, sign myself

SPENCER T. HALL,

"The Sherwood Forester."

Burnley, July 10th, 1877.

INDEX.

—o—

PENDLE HILL

AND

ITS SURROUNDINGS.

CHAPTER I.

A MAY-TIDE PILGRIMAGE.

" The love of Nature—the fondness for retiring
at times to her loneliest scenes—exists among
us all in various degrees. . . . And if you
have learnt to think of the creation, not as ended,
but as still going on, not as once done then left
to the care of a distant Providence, but as being
every moment subject to the renewing influences
of a present God, you will readily understand
why the human soul is brought into communion
with Him when amid the lonely scenes of this
beautiful world."—Professor H. N. GRIMLEY, in
" *Tremadoc Sermons.*"

IT was a bright and sweet May morning.
The lark was pouring its rill of song
from above, the cuckoo " counting time "
with its double note below; the lane
banks were glistening with buttercups, neighbours
now and then to the primrose and violet, more
rare, but not less dear. The leafing hedges and
bushes were half hiding the building birds and
their little mansions ; and way-side wells were
murmuring forth their gentle music—in short,
all nature seemed giving eyes and ears to the
heart—as I passed away from Colne by the foot
of Black How (or Bleak How, which is it ?)

down to Roughlee, in "Pendle Forest." And
every step I took made me more in love with
natural and popular names, as distinct from
those derived merely from books. Far up before
me "Pendle Hill," wooer of winds and parent
of streams, cleft the heavens to the height of
1,850 feet or so above the level of the sea on
which in the far distance it looks; and "Pendle-
water,"—now rushing and gurgling, now flowing
less rapidly and whispering "sermons in the
stones" on its floor, cheered me on towards the
pastoral and tufted slopes of Roughlee; and the
whole scene told me that this was not *Pendle*, but
Pen-Dale.

There can be no doubt that the old Cymric
Pen—the hill—presiding over the scene, conferred
the honour of its name on all below. Hence the
beautiful strath I was entering had become
Pen-dale, its rivulet Pen-dale Water, the end of
that dale below Brierfield, *many a mile away from
the bottom of the hill*, Pen-dale Bottom; while the
whole space through which it ran was called
Pen-dale (shortened by time and custom to *Pendle*)
Forest. All this was natural and perfectly accor-
dant with popular logic and convenience. When
the Saxons, Danes and Normans came, they found
and recognised the old British name of *Pen*, as
they found Pen-y-Ghent, Helvellyn, and Skidaw,
and would have had no occasion to be discontented
with this more than with those names; but having
to designate the dale, with the water, the forest,
and other objects, in reference and deference to
the mountain-chief, there grew in time, by natural
reaction, a tendency in nomenclature to distinguish the mountain from the vales and forests at
its feet, the waters thence flowing away, and their
kindred, to all of which it had "stood sponsor,"
by calling it in return Pen-hull or Pen-hill, the *d*

belonging to the *dale*, in the first instance, and
not to the hill, except by inadvertance. I know
that some hypercritics, backed by such venerated
authorities as Whitaker and Wilkinson, will come
down upon me with a leaden thud for starting
this hypothesis, and will ask why the hill should
be called by the same name on all sides. To this
objection *in prospectu* I would answer that as the
old forest-courts were held at Higham, on the
south side of the hill, whatever name was given to
it there would, as a matter of course, gradually
extend to all the rest of the domain. At all events
let my opinion, derived from careful reading,
observation, and many popular analogies, be taken
as I have ventured it, just for what it is worth;
it may not, on consideration, be found altogether
valueless. But we will now proceed.

There is a rich little world for the geologist,
the botanist, the ornithologist, or the entomologist
in the next few hundred yards after leaving
"Blackow Foot." The winding rivulet, with its
rock-paved and pebble-strown bottom; its mossy,
rooty, shrubby, and primrosed banks; the rough-
wooded "brae" on yonder side, the enclosed
pastures on this, with their bleating ewes, fresh-
yeaned lambs, and watchful shepherds; the flitting
insects and piping birds—how blessèd all! And
now Roughlee hamlet, its gabled and mullioned
old hall, and many another antique homestead,
are reached, and one ponders awhile there. These
two farmers I fall in with are glad of a little
gossip, and I of their information, as we come to
the conclusion that Mrs. Nutter, who some two
hundred years ago was condemned to die for
"witchcraft" practised here, probably far trans-
cended her accusers in every humane quality;
that there is not the less interest in the sight of
one of the neighbouring houses now declining

that some of the intelligent Greenwoods, of Burnley, had ancestry there; that the distinguished
and enlightened founder of the Hartley Institute
at Southampton, a relative of theirs, was born not
far off; that one of my intelligent acquaintance
went a-courting to yon upland cottage in his
youth, and met with a droll adventure one night
in leaping a hedge when returning; and many
other touches of the mystical, grotesque, or genial,
suitable to such a primitive rural realm.

As to Witchcraft: wonder and imagination are
human faculties, and will always find exercise in
accordance with the spheres of the possessors,
their life, surroundings, and relative development.
Where natural things are not understood there is
mostly a tendency to account for them preter-
naturally or supernaturally, if not unnaturally.
Hence, in days when what are now called mesmerism and electro-biology had not shown (to
use an old ironical sceptic's joke) how, by peculiar
sympathy or antipathy, "one person's mind could
move another person's muscles," there often, and
chiefly in obscure localities, occurred effects—
queer illusions among them—which were attri-
buted to good or evil spirits, and greatly exaggerated by report. In these, at one time, it is said,
Pendle Forest abounded; and so long as the law
recognised and punished all "witchcraft" as
devilishness, nothing was more easy than for a wanton or malignant person to heap odium even on the
best of neighbours by imputing to them possession
and exercise of the power. It was thus, it is now
believed, that Mrs. Nutter, of Roughlee Hall,
and many others, were belied and sentenced to
death at Lancaster, partly through the subsequently
confessed subornation of a young boy named
Edmund Robinson. As to the much quoted con-
fession of Margret Johnson, of which a full account

is given in books specially treating on such subjects; having often seen in late years, by what is at present called " electro-biology," people deluded into believing themselves steam-engines, tigers, dogs, cats, &c. (a sort of pastime by no means to be recommended), I should refer the statements in most confessions of witchcraft to a similar cause; and as a remedy, give the people something better wherewith to occupy their minds.

Going along, I could soon see where William Dugdale read his first lessons in geology, and why Joseph Whitaker was once so fond of coming hither from Burnley to ponder on the same, and collect specimens with him, which they found abounding in the shale. Leaves of stone interlapping each other finely pave the bed of Pendlewater there, and these again over-scattered by a sort of boulder-stones, some small as a farthing, others large as a hippopotamus, and in much the same shapes, must have awakened rare delight in the mind of Dugdale when he was young; and I mused on them, and him in relation to them, while lingering there, as several of his old neighbours pointed out to me the places where he had dwelt, and spoke of him and his *originality* with kindliest respect. Both here and a little higher up the dale, at " Narrow-Yates," are manufactories and the usual accompaniments of operatives' dwellings, chapels and schools, but interfering little with the primitive character of the locality or its natural picturesqueness. How the whole scene reminded me of Edale, in Derbyshire!

All this was very pleasing, but much as it preoccupied did not incapacitate me for a fresh burst of rural delight on coming to Mr. Farrer's cheerful mansion at Thorneyholme, overlooked by the tall column of a factory chimney it is true, but sentinelling the opening into sweet meadows

beyond, that win beauty to beauty as they extend
to Whitehough, the seat of Mr. Bollard, near
Barley.

Of Barley I had often heard or read, and was
not surprised to find it as rustic and yet as
recherché in some respects as it proved to be.
The narrowing, but still clear and musical stream,
here joined by one not less copious from Ogden,
and both fed by many a limpid wayside well; the
humble but not despisable hostelrie called the
" Pendle Inn ; " the tall old rookery and more
imposing homestead by its side " over the way ; "
the radiating lanes, here called " loins," and footpaths ; the clusterings and scatterings of more
humble dwellings in every direction, all helped to
tell me into what a remote " nook of the world "
—remote from all its turmoil, din, and smoke—
I had penetrated ; while grand old Pendle incited
me to closer acquaintance with him and invited me
to climb his throne.

In the course of my walk I had inquired of
several the probable amount of fatigue and cost of
time should I venture the ascent, and was dis-
couraged by all, considering my apparent years
and weight, till reaching Barley. It there became
clear to me that those who dwelt nearest made
lightest of any difficulty in climbing the hill. I
had come from Blackow Foot, not above three or
four miles, lunching at Thorneyholme by the way,
and it was now not more than three o'clock.
Numbers of people who had been up were already
descending, and ascertaining that some of them
had accomplished both the rise and descent in as
few hours as yet remained of daylight, my resolve
was soon taken to emulate them. A lame but
plucky and intelligent boy of seventeen, son of a
widow at Narrow Yates, who said he had often
been up, engaged to accompany me ; and I thought

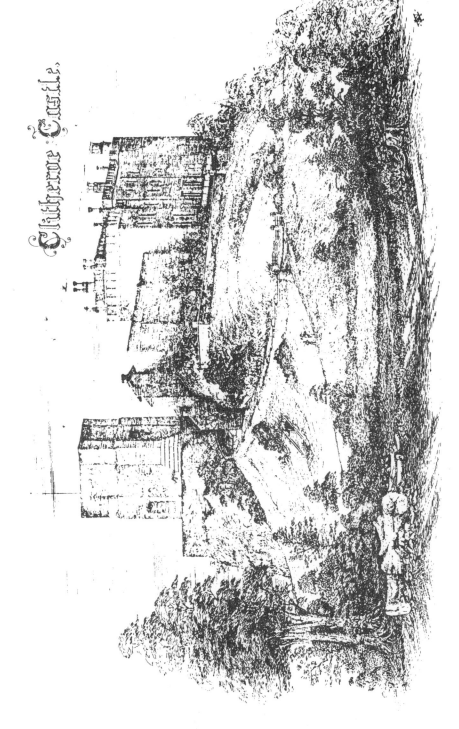

Clitheroe Castle.

Bolton-by-Bolland Church.

Crowland Abbey.

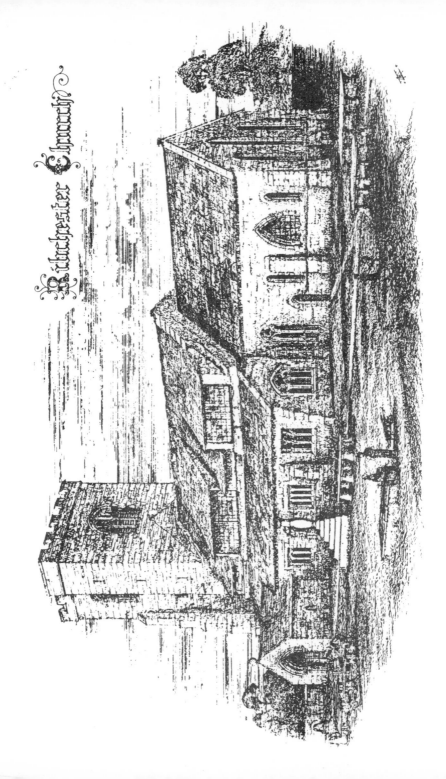

Ribchester Church

if *he* could accomplish it, it could be no great
hardship for me.

It was a "good step," however, from the village
to the mountain foot, occupying little less than
half-an-hour, yet an enjoyable walk, with the
music of many rills and "rindles" as Samuel
Bamford would have called them, by the way.
On nearing the steep we paused awhile to estimate
our chances. Two courses were open, and
my young companion was ready for either. My
object being to reach the beacon-stones at the
highest point as soon as possible, could this best
be done by taking the long-winding cart-road to
the left, or, at my time of life, braving the
mountain's breast a little on our right? We at
length undertook the latter, but much to our regret
long ere we reached the summit. There had been
many weeks of dry weather; the turf and heather
were very slippery to tread or cling to, and the
firing of some ling to the windward not only sent
about us a cloud of smoke, baffling our sight a
little, but from its proximity threatening us if we
rested with positive danger. Yet, in less than an
hour-and-a-half from leaving Barley, our point
was gained. Two gentlemen, the one from Barrowford, the other from Fulshaw, who had started
at the same time as ourselves, but by the cart-
road, rough though winding as it is, had greatly
the advantage of us; and I should advise all
future visitors, not ambitious of dislocating their
shoulders or breaking their necks, to imitate them
and not us in the climb. Yet ours was not without *some* compensation. It gave us a more effective
view at several points, as we paused and gazed
down into the primitive and pastoral life of the
dale and minor hills, and made the conquest more
consoling to me as a test of my remaining power
as a climber, after a cessation for many years of

such pastimes.   Little more than a year before I
had descended 280 yards into Bank-hall coal-pit,
and penetrated its workings for half-a-mile ; since
that, though more than sixty-three years old, and
above fifteen stones in weight, had leaped the
" Strid " in Bolton woods ; and now, at sixty-four,
had mounted " old Pendle" on its steepest and
slipperiest side—in none of those cases for *èclat*—
that never entered my head, but from a very
different motive ; and I am not sure but that its
result has made me feel. younger by many years
than before, so far as the physical power which I
had once partially lost, and which providentially
is now restored, is concerned.

George Fox, founder of the Society of Friends, or
Quakers, coming up from the neighbourhood of
Bradford into these parts, in the year 1652, says
under that date in his published journal, " As we
travelled we came near a very great high hill,
called Pendle Hill, and I was moved of the Lord
to go up to the top of it, which I did with much
ado, it was so very steep and high.   When I came
to the top I saw the sea bordering on Lancashire.
From the top of this hill the Lord let me see in
what places he had a great people to be gathered.
As I went down I found a spring of water in the
side of the hill, with which I refreshed myself,
having eaten or drunk but little several days
before.   At night we came to an inn, and declared
truth to the man of the house, and wrote a paper
to the priests and professors, declaring the Day of
the Lord, and that Christ was come to teach
people himself, by His power and spirit in their
hearts.   *   *   *   The man of the house spread
the paper abroad, and was himself mightily affected
with the truth.   Here the Lord opened to me to
see a great people in white raiment by a river
side coming to the Lord.   *   *   *   The next day

we travelled on, and at night got a little fern to
put under us, and lay upon a common." I believe
it was about the same time that this wonderful
man, in a state that might perhaps not irreverently
be termed clairvoyant, saw the relation of things
external to internal humanity in such a way as to
make him think of becoming a physician, but that
it was then shown him he had a more spiritual
duty to perform. It is certain that after this experience there was a great accession to his fraternity
in the Yorkshire dales. .

Nearly all agree that just after sunrise or before
sunset is the best time for contemplating the views
from Pendle-top; and perhaps I cannot give a
better idea of my own impressions than in the
following verses, flung off by myself at Burnley a
short time before :—

TO PENDLE HILL.

More like a living creature stretch'd in sleep,
Its couch the forest and its cope the sky,
Than of geology's rich boasts a heap,
To me thou seem'st in thy repose to lie,
Though with a changing physiognomy,
According with the varying light and shade
That to the heart send music through the eye,
By morn, or eve, or melting moonlight made,
Or seasons in their different panoplies arrayed.

Whether when winter clothes in spotless white,
Or springtide tints thy sides with living green,
Or summer crowns thy summit with its light
And lends thy purpling heather heavenly sheen,
Or autumn's riper grandeur gilds the scene,
Great Pendle ! in thy dignity alone,
Thou reignest matchless over moor and dene,—
A monarch owing not to man thy throne, ;
Yet making regal all around thy footstool strown.

How glorious 'tis, old king ! to be with thee
Taking thy view of all the vast expanse,—
Towns, towers, farms, fields, mansions, and distant
   sea,—

Some seeming to retreat and some advance,
Now shunning and now seeking poet's glance,
Or painter's, who must here be Nature's thrall
And give his spirit up to her romance,
Wishing within his raptured heart that all
Her votaries could come and share it at his call!

I come, for one, and with me gladly bring
The region's native laureate*—calm yet strong ;—
Or brings he me, to hear him aptly sing
Again in words thy breeze and skylark's song ?—
Or am I only *dreaming* here, among
Black Burnley's rattling looms and clouds of smoke ?—
Yet why the soft illusion not prolong ?
For it is not " a melancholy joke "—
A frail and fleeting spell, no sooner felt than broke.

No, massive mountain ! let me, as I see
Ev'n from this dingy street thy outlines bold,
Come, and with feelings fresh and fancy free
With sunshine or with storm communion hold,
Thinking of others who in days of old
Made thee for war or worship their abode,
And left some traces that we might be told
How not alone by moderns thou art trod,
While those who scaled thee erst felt not less near to God !

George Fox, the Quaker prophet, sought thy brow
To commune with the MIGHTY SPIRIT there,
And then descended to the crowds below,
An earnest war with cant and crime to dare ;—
And who can tell how many a child of care
And toil from thee hath calm and courage caught,
Enabling him to take a champion's share
In service that by gold could ne'er be bought—
Men of bold act as well as of unfetter'd thought ?

And hear we not the telling names that linger,
Alter'd or pure, of objects all around,
While hoary Time lifts to his ear his finger,
As listening with delight the far-come sound—
As though it told of olden friends re-found ?
Whernside, and Inglebro', and Pen-y-Ghent,
And Colne—of Saxon, Celt, and Roman speak ;
And rivulets with quaint names, their voices blent,
Call echoes down from woodland, cliff, and peak,
Waking fresh bloom in age's pale and wrinkled cheek.

---

* Henry Houlding, author of " In the Wood," and of many other
beautiful poems.

But—*Pendle Witches!* Ah, there still are plenty,
If kindly look and voice can make them so;—
A single man might soon find twelve or twenty
Who, were he young, could work him mickle woe;—
Not of the wild, weird sort that long ago
Spread superstitious terror far and wide,
But damsels virtuous, and chaste as snow,
The Forest's admiration, hope, and pride,
Which one the best to love 'twould tax him to decide!

And though brisk manufacture taints our sky
Six days together with its smoke unburn'd,
Upon the sev'nth it giveth to the eye
A thousand obelisks,—as if it mourn'd
What it had done to nature, and so turn'd
On sabbaths to an Oriental clime
Of classic columns all the chimnied land,—
A scene of human interests sublime
As any ever known in thy old annals, Time!

How pleasant 'tis to see so finely blending
The various signs of Nature and of art,
That, though our trade is more and more extending,
Good taste fulfils throughout the land its part,
And life displays at once both mind and heart!
While wood and moor fade out, the garden grows;
As ancient beauties vanish, new ones start;
As fails the wilding, flourisheth the rose;
And for the vapid marsh the factory lakelet glows.

Nay! what is art itself but Nature, shown
Through human agency—a second birth?
And where the seed of ages past was sown
New forms of things, yet in accord, come forth.
'Tis thus that changes beautify the earth.
Ev'n contrast reconciles the old and new;
But for new fabrics what were ruins worth?
Bringing fresh thought and enterprise to view,
The present and the past the future see imbue!

Lo! how the winding Ribble westward wends
To meet at Preston Lytham's up-sent tide;
While eastward Craven's pastoral realm extends
Near where the Aire and Wharfe and Wenning glide,
And Malham Cove and Gordale Scar just hide;

B

As southward Boulsworth bleak o'er Hebden looks,
And Blackstone Edge melts in the skies away,
And woods wave welcome to the birth of brooks;
While the West-Calder comes to Whalley grey,
And Clitheroe's Keep hails heights that watch far More-
      cambe Bay !

But let us not o'erlook the pleasant spots
Cluster'd, or scatter'd, nearer to thy feet :
Fair Downham with its hall, or Worston's cots,
Or Sabden's church and stream and cheerful street,
Where Richard Cobden once found sweet retreat,
Nursing the thoughts that now bless half mankind;—
Or glance we back to Stonyhurst, learning's seat,
Albeit to its ritual not confined,
But where the youth who are may chastest teaching find.

Gaze where we may, the whole so fresh and fair—
The vales and plains beneath, the heavens above—
The marks of good abounding everywhere—
Tell the old story of a God of Love.
The rocks and hills stand fast, the waters move ;
The sunlit clouds with gladsome breezes play ;
The meadows green set off the dusky grove ;
Where ruminate the herds, the lambs are gay ;
While Eden dawns again, so lovely is the day.

And now, O GREAT SUPREME ! we turn to THEE,
Who in Thy robe of light o'er all dost reign :—
What a grand miracle it is to be,
(Dear Lord of sky and mountain, vale and plain !)
Gifted with mind to learn and to retain
Some little lore, both natural and divine,
Or tell it to each other o'er again,
As though 'twere ours, while yet it is but Thine,
In Thy great goodness given to win us to Thy shrine.

At that pure shrine with reverence let us bow—
Not that Thou needest our poor prayer, or praise,
But, Father ! that our sense of Thee 'twill show—
To ask Thy help the low and lost to raise,
From errors of the past, in coming days—
To let them look on Nature's face and see
Thy love reflected there ; and make our ways
With our best knowledge evermore agree,
And all the world feel blest and comforted in Thee !

Burnley, April, 1877.

Yet how little can a few verses convey of all that reaches the mind here! What strange and stirring histories have been enacted in this wide arena! If it be true, as science has ventured to say, that all which transpires in a room is recorded in "invisible ink" on its walls till some future day, what a book there must be hidden within the grasp of this horizon! What struggles for power and battles for liberty, and for real or imagined right, if regarded for such events alone! Tracings in old archives and on canvas by the human hand are nothing to this. The British prelude, the Roman occupation, the Danish invasions, the Saxon and Norman strife, the Yorkist and Lancastrian lust and rage for the possession of a throne, painful and unsafe when gained; the great Royalist and Parliamentarian crisis, when the amazon Countess of Derby (persecutor of the poor Quakers) so long defended Lathom Hall as it was besieged, and scarcely a mouthful of provender was left, on which she occasioned noises as of pig-killing, day by day, to dishearten the besiegers and make them believe she could still stand firm and secure, till they were tired out! Prince Charles Stuart coming across yon hill with his army of Scotchmen in hope of restoring his fallen house; while down in the opposite plain brave Towneley raised and led forth the only English regiment that dared to join them, for which he was executed;—in short, an epitome of the whole political and feudal history of the land;—how reflected to the mind, as we gaze and muse!

Nor less the strange mosaic of ecclesiastical and civil life, including the Pilgrimage of Grace, so called, for wresting back from the grip of Henry the power of the Church—a movement in which John Paslew, the last abbot of Whalley, took a

conspicuous, yet failing and fatal part; Jollie, the
Puritan preacher, in turn dragged by soldiers
from Healey Hall and imprisoned for many years,
and now a monumental chapel erected to his
memory in the little hamlet of Barrow just below
us, the latter chiefly, I believe, through the influ-
ence of Mr. Foster, J.P., of the Whins, and Mr.
Bryce Smith; the old Church called Established,
by no means yet blotted out, while the elder Church
of Rome seems positively reviving, though Dissent
is permeating every nook of the land, and free
thought and free expression of it may everywhere
be heard. But, as wondrous as any of the rest,
is this mighty growth of manufacturing skill and
wealth in what once must have been one of the
most naked, dreary, and impoverished parts of the
kingdom!

These, and a thousand times as much (were
there but space and time to embrace all) might
occupy one long on a spot like this. But the con-
sciousness of *Unseen Good* aróund, the calm sky
above, and the thought of those myriads of " other
worlds" still hidden in light, win us anon from
all merely sublunary things, until we feel lost in
the mystery of existence, yet, despite all anomalous
seemings, have a grateful

                              " sense
Of that which is of all Creator and Defence."

Whalley Abbey.

—·— Entrance Gateway. —·—

Whalley Abbey.

ONE OF THE SOUTH WEST ANGLES

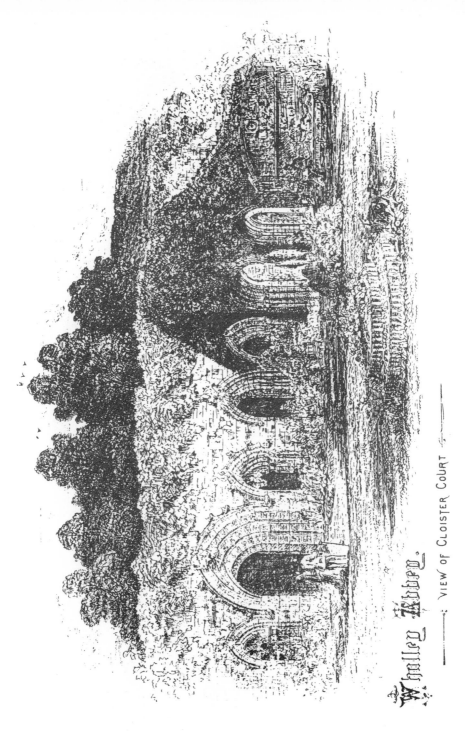

Whalley Abbey.

: VIEW OF CLOISTER COURT :

Whalley Church.

CHAPTER II.

The Return.

AS the day went softly and beautifully down on one side the mountain, I and my unwearied though crippled cicerone came down on the other—often stopping to *listen the sabbath silence*, as it were, to inspire the calm yet refreshing air, and take in the still fair though fading scene. It was growing dusk when we overtook the two strong climbers from the forest, whom we had seen and parted with at starting. It was too late for me to return, as was at first intended, to Brierfield, and catch the evening train for Burnley; but there was recompense for this in a friendly conversation, a frugal supper, and a snug and clean though homely bed at the little inn.

After a good, if plain, breakfast next morning, and a cheery chat with the host and his family, I went with him as far as the entrance to Ogden Clough—he on his way round by the "Buttocks" to Clitheroe, and I by a short upland. curve to NEWCHURCH. But before reaching that place it was a gratification to pause awhile, leaning over a gate or stile, to re-contemplate all I had enjoyed and was now leaving. Spout House, a white gleaming mansion, the residence of a friend, Mr. Holroyd Bolton, towards the Moorcock, from which I had descended yestermorn, seemed still to be keeping some connection with me over the far-stretching and undulating vale; and as I gazed

high at the now sun-bright *Pen*, more near, a
remembrance of its solemn aspect the night
before, as I had looked up and seen it in its
majesty wearing a diadem of stars, came on me.
And then the *human life* below—the rural homes,
the peaceful industry, the few ascending sounds,
all came so genially into my soul that I could not
help (metaphorically speaking) putting them in
my bosom and blessing them on passing away.

And now for curious, quaint, quiet, grey little
Newchurch—which, notwithstanding its name,
might almost seem emulant of Pendle itself in
antiquity. And remember, it is not Newchurch
at, or *by*, or *near*, but *in* Pendle—that possible
abbreviation, as already hinted, of *Pen-dale*, as
another place is called Newchurch-*in*-Rossendale.
One might almost fancy from the look of this
Newchurch (or Newkirk, as it is more generally
called in the locality) that, despite its name, it
never had been new—reminding one of that
mayor of Shrewsbury, sitting by a judge in the
town-hall there and saying, in reply to his lordship's remark that it seemed a very ancient place,
" it *always was*, my lord ! "

Old inns, ten times older than teetotalism ;
shops differing in importance, where you might
expect to purchase anything—from a side of bacon
down to " coffee, tea, tobacco, snuff, train oil,
treacle, nails, and whipcord ; " door-steps, as convenient to tumble from as to climb ; and scarcely
a person in the street to answer a question as to
whereto it might lead ; yet not without many
superior touches of cleanliness and respectability
withal : such were the outlines imprinted on me
as I sought the church itself, and pleasant parsonage by its side. The only thing in the village
appearing at all " new " was the ample school
that has recently started up for company to these

retired and partially embowered fabrics, and from which the subdued hum of childhood's morning exercises came as I drew near.

The good clergyman, the Rev. J. H. Horrox, M.A., was away that day; but an obliging domestic enlisted the sexton's wife to unlock a door of the neat " chapel," with its one-belled tower, its clean and open sittings, its organ aloft and church-warden's seats (four or five in one pew), and a pretty though diminutive baptismal font, below; an old funereal monument out of sight, a new and neat modern marble one on the southern wall; the plain but convenient pulpit, desks, and enrailed com-munion table, overlooked by the usual inscriptions of the Lord's Prayer, Decalogue and Apostles' Creed, from the walls of the modest chancel; with the solemn stillness and the in-gleamings of morning sunshine—all made me thankful for my little stay, and not less at peace with God and man, or less in love with old English simplicity, on my de-parture.

The first chapel was erected here by the inhabi-tants of the five booths of Gouldshaw, Barley, Whitley, Roughlee, and Ouldlawnde, of which the sentence of consecration, by John Bird, the first Bishop of Chester, bears date Oct. 1, 1544.

It would have been an easy and agreeable walk to return to Burnley, viâ Fence and Brierfield; or to have stretched round by Higham and the old Sparrow Hawk in Wheatley-lane. But I com-pleted a sort of circuit by walking across the fields to that home of taste, Carr Hall, that within has many artistic, as around it has many natural, charms; and striking through Nelson back to Colne,—thus completing what altogether made one of the most enjoyable rural excursions imaginable.

CHAPTER III.

OTHER POINTS AND APPROACHES.

ANY party wishing to reach Pendle from Burnley entirely on foot, might properly start on the Colne-road, turn down Byerden-lane, and find the way to New-church through Fence. If not averse to a semi-circuit, it might to many be more interesting to go up by the Sparrow Hawk (a famous hostelrie in olden days), and Higham, alluded to in the previous chapter, but of which something more ought to be said. It is a large, old-fashioned village, straggling along and rather high up the country side, as its name may imply. The forest-courts were once, and are still sometimes, held there, of which various relics and remarkable traditions remain—the spot being yet pointed out where offenders against the forest laws under the Anglo-Norman regime sometimes were hanged. On first passing through this place, I was struck by its likeness to another of the same name, and like it too called *Hig-ham*, on the line of the old Roman road from Little Chester to Chesterfield, in Derbyshire.

Amongst the many things to note at Higham-in-Pendle is an ancient public-house called "The Four Alls," where the "Almote Courts" are still held—having a sign on which are painted the portraits of a clergyman, a king, a soldier and a farmer, the first saying "I pray for all;" the second, "I govern all;" the third, "I fight for all;" the fourth, "I

pay for all!" Benjamin Moore, who was born
there, will some day probably tell you more about
this interesting old village.

But one of the prettiest walks in England—
and especially from Nelson or Colne—would be
to go some fine day down to Barrowford, "the
little Manchester of the Forest," where, however,
the great mills of Mr. Barrowclough and other
important works are soon left behind and out of
sight as you turn up by the water-side path, noting
the picturesque one-arched old bridge and the
half-retired domain of Crowtrees, property of a
branch of the Grimshaw family, as you pass along.
There are some exquisite " vignettes " for a good
sketcher in that quarter. And as you go on by
Utherstone and the Water-meetings, you will soon
be struck by the great peculiarity of the rising
landscape, not unakin to scenes in the Peak of
Derbyshire. Pen-dale may not necessarily have
taken its name from the one great hill alone. The
whole forest here being so undulating, it might
not inaptly, if you will admit such logic, be called
a *dale of pens*, abounding with fine projections and
knolls, some wooded and cotted and some naked,
like Brown-hill and Black-how for instance,—*the*
chief Pen, in his sublime repose, looking calmly,
solemnly, and somewhat patriarchally down on all.
And soon, still meeting the clear and rippling
river, you reach Roughlee and Barley, described
before.

Near the entrance to Barrowford from the Nelson
side, you see on the right Reedy-ford, the attractive
seat of Mr. Tunstill, by which Colne-brook comes
round with low musical voice to woo Pendle-water.
Give it a good look, for it is a pretty scene. And
you will afterwards find the long village street
ever and anon relieved by some home of taste, as
you pass ; a villa over the fields may awake to your

remembrance the late well-known Alderman Hiram
Uttley, J.P., who partially resided there ; and the
little church and parsonage near it, in the same
direction, will long be associated with the venerated
name of the late Rev. Samuel Smith, M.A., a good
man, who lived in the hearts of all the parish, as
all the parish lived in his heart ; while several
other pleasant residences will give you a "God-
speed" sort of smile about the far end of the
village as you stroll on.

Another interesting but rather arduous way to
Pendle is through Padiham and Sabden, by "Red
Rock." The derivation of the name of Padiham
has been the subject of many a joke, but the irregu-
larly built town itself is very fast becoming one of
importance in manufactures and trade ; and it is
now so easy to arrive at it by train or omnibus
from Burnley, as it looks up at the darkening
Hambledon Hills, or out towards Accrington,
Blackburn, and Preston, that even a devout pedes-
trian would scarcely have an excuse for not riding
to Padiham. Afterwards, the upper right hand
road from Padiham to Sabden, by the "Red Rock,"
would be well worth taking for many reasons.
For a considerable distance it is a rare old English
lane, with lofty, rugged banks, and handsome trees
here and there in the hedge-rows, running along
or bending from their tops ; while the views, on
looking aside or back—including one of Gawthorpe
Hall, the seat of Sir Ughtred Kay-Shuttleworth,
Bart., M.P., whose late accomplished and public-
spirited father, Sir James, has left some graphic
descriptions of the neighbourhood, its life and
character—are far-reaching and picturesque.

At length, pursuing this course and leaving
Higham at some distance out of sight on the
right, one of the loveliest little views in England
suddenly bursts on the eye—that of Sabden, the

name originally derived from verbal roots meaning
a sandy or sand-streaked vale; but with its now
green and golden growths of pasture, bower, and
flower; its pleasant mansions and clean though
humble cottages, scattered or in rows; its church
and chapels, schools, mills, meadows, and clear
water-gleams, with lofty Pendle striking up in the
back-ground from left to right; while deep and
rugged Ogden Clough lies hid between it and a
nearer ridge, which is itself no mean eminence;
speak of anything but sterility or sandiness there
in the ordinary sense. The names of Cobden and
Foster, with those of other worthies, are pleasantly
associated with Sabden and its history. I have
been told that Cobden manifested a special interest
in its schools whilst occasionally residing there;
and take the valley for all in all, the whole scene
is so cheerful yet so calm, that a poet of the
James Hurnard or William Brockie type might
well wish to live and die in such a spot. There
is a road from Sabden to the lower end of Pendle
Hill direct.

Yet perhaps as interesting and in the main as
easy a way as any is the turnpike road from
Padiham towards Whalley, striking between sunny
and sylvan Huntroyd, seat of the Starkie family,
and Symonstone, another picturesque place just
glimpsing through the glade, connected historically
with the same patrician name, but the residence
I believe now of Mr. William Dugdale. Mr.
Dixon, a literary excursionist from Ormskirk,
was delighted here; and no wonder; for the
views hence grow constantly more magnificent,
varied, and delightful, as we advance. Up on
the right strikes the fair domain of Read Hall,
and down on the left the West Calder keeps
stealing into then vanishing from sight, as if
playing at hide-and-seek with its own naiads;

steep-wooded slopes and pastures dipping down
to it from every side as it glides, till anon we
come upon Whalley, its grey and ample village,
its old church, and far-famed Abbey ruins.   Let
us linger awhile on their history.

It has long been a maxim with me not to believe
all that the enemies of persons, sects, parties, any
more than of nations, say against them, without
first taking as calm a look as possible on the other
side.   Hence, whenever I hear it sneeringly said
of the old monks, that they showed selfishness and
love of luxury for its own sake, in the choice of
retired and beautiful spots for the sites of their
houses, I always hypothetically take a view of the
possible condition of those spots before, and
of any kindly reasons for their settling there.
I dare say they make a cosy sort of home, even
now, in that lofty Alpine cleft of St. Bernard;
but what would it be without them?   War, and
warlike defence, nearly always in old England
sought the craggy hill; humility and love of
abstract meditation just as naturally sought the
vale, whereto all sorts of people might have easy
access for sharing the devotions, instruction,
hospitality, and solace there, apart from the
ostentatiousness of feudal power and love of battle.
But the early monks must often have found the
places of their retreat rough enough at starting.

I was born near to Newstead Abbey, in Notts,
and could easily see what a miserable series of
marshes, overlooked by sterile sandy hills, that
place must have been ere the monks came to
reclaim it; yet how beautiful now!   And any
one who goes to lovely Tintern may yet see, in
passing between its most elegant abbey ruins
and the village, what a mere bog the whole dell
must once have been.   And not only has many
a marsh been drained, but many a hard rock

subdued, by pious industry. In my own time,
the most bleak and sterile part of Charnwood
Forest, near Sheep-shed, Leicestershire, has been
turned into garden, farm, and reformatory for
criminal boys, by a Roman Catholic brotherhood,
who call the place Mount St. Bernard.

So possibly of Whalley as a retreat in foul times
from feudal animosity, tyranny, and riot.   An oft-
flooded and marshy meadow it must once have
been. It is clear the desert must have been much
redeemed by industry ere it could " blossom as the
rose," notwithstanding it was called " Locus Benedictus," in contrast to the wretched place they
relinquished for it.   The passing Calder, no doubt,
afforded a good fry of fish in Lent, and a contri-
bution of venison from the proximate forest might
occasionally reach them at other times ; but it
could not have become the luxuriant and luxurious
scene of later time, without much patience and
labour first.   Could any one really think it was
made even what we see it now without the axe,
" spud," spade and fork having been most assi-
duously and regularly plied ?   And if at length its
pater familias by virtue of accessions of territory
and some court, grew into the proud " Lord
Abbot," of one thing we may be sure, those
accessions would never have been made but for
somebody believing the institution worthy of them.
It is customary with the moderns to speak of the
ancients with too much ingratitude and contempt.
It is impossible now to tell all the good we may
owe to them. For myself, when climbing any
of the surrounding hills, I cannot but think
with some respect, if not reverence, of the ancient
Druids—missionaries from the Eastern Magi—
the " wise men from the East,"—who once worshipped the One God here, and who never, so far
as we know, opposed the coming of Christianity,

though some of their heathen persecutors did;
and, then, of those Monks down in the vale superseding them in time in their functions of teachers,
healers, and softeners of the rudeness and ferocity
of all around them, until they partly wore out
their *true* power by departing from their original
simplicity and piety, and invited the rapacity of
Henry VIII and his myrmidons, by too ostenta-
tiously displaying their wealth. It is not impossible,
perhaps, that Cardinal Wolsey, who was himself
practically about as much a layman as an eccle-
siastic, unwittingly had done something to thus
provoke the national visitation that so soon followed him.   Let us not altogether forget this view
of things while gazing on the now dismembered
and crumbling relics of Whalley Abbey.

It was by a migration from Stanlaw, in Cheshire,
a miserable and comparatively unimprovable place,
commenced in the year 1172, that the Cistertian
Brotherhood, to whom it belonged, obtained a
steading, which they called "Locus Benedictus,"
here. In this we are told they encountered the
jealousy and hostility of the neighbouring Abbey
of Salley-on-the-Ribble, and some other local
difficulties; but having pitched their little encampment, they maintained their ground, and
grew for upwards of 300 years.   Their territories,
especially in pasturage, were very extensive, including no inconsiderable part of Rossendale; but
it is notorious (see Whitaker) that because of their
unbounded hospitality and generosity in many
ways, *they were never rich,* and seldom out of debt.

It appears that at one time women, under the
name of recluses, were allowed residence here;
but some of them became wanton and led such
lives, that the more pious of the fraternity peti-
tioned for their removal, which was accomplished.

John Paslew was the last Abbot of Whalley;

and, according to Whitaker, must have been as
hospitable and worthy a man as most of his pre-
decessors.   But no matter, when the harsh decrees
of Henry VIII. rang out, he, like many others,
became rebellious because dispossessed, and after
joining in the "Pilgrimage of Grace," was tried
for treason at Lancaster, and executed near the
spot where he was born.   Whatever one's creed, it
is hardly possible not to sympathise somewhat
with his fidelity to his own Order, and with a
rhymer, who has said :—

> "Whalley's last Abbot claims at least a thought :
> Of evils two 'tis best to choose not one,
> Is very true; but as by arms he sought
> To make bold Henry for his greed atone,
> And then was by his confreres left alone,
> 'Twas hard, when gone was all his zeal and hope,
> To find no mercy in that heart of stone,
> Which sentenced to the strangulating rope
> One who so long had worn the sacerdotal cope."

This little book is not one in which to go much
further into historical detail.   For that let me
refer you to a discriminative reading of Whitaker,
Roby, and Baines ; for architectural information
and illustration to W. A. Waddington's tasteful
book, "Sketches on the Calder and the Ribble in
and around Whalley ; " and for romantic legend
to Harland, Wilkinson, and W. H. Ainsworth.
And there is, I am told, another very interesting
work, which I deeply regret having not yet seen,
entitled "Rambles by the Ribble," by W. Dobson.

Mr. Edgar Appleby at present resides in what
of the abbey is still habitable, and I feel sure that
either he or the vicar, the Rev. R. N. Whitaker,
M.A., (son of the historian, I believe,) has a
pleasure in giving information to any tasteful
visitor.

It is not far from Whalley that the Calder and

the Hodder fall into the Ribble as it bends thither-
wards.   Mitton Church and the celebrated Roman
Catholic College of Stoneyhurst—one near, the
other more than a mile away—helping to enhance
the interest of all around ; and there are many
views both on the Ribble and Hodder beyond all
description, exquisite.   Sawley ruins, a favourite
resort, are near, on the Ribble, beyond Chatburn ;
and here is a sweet little scene on the Hodder :—

Near Whitewell.

From Whalley it will be tolerably easy to find
a route up by Wiswell to Pendle Hill.   Or, if you
can command time, and the weather be favourable,
run up to Clitheroe by rail, take a good look at
the quaint borough and its ancient and elevated
castle, belonging to the Duke of Buccleuch, as
Lord of the " Honour ;" but occupied by **Mr.**
Dixon Robinson, as agent for the same, in all its
vast extent, including Burnley.   There will also be
much besides to see.   And then you can pass on
by Chatburn to Worston and Downham, with a
detour to the ruins of Sawley Abbey if you are

driving, or can stay the night. To give an index to the antique usages of Clitheroe, I may specify one :—Going a few years ago along one of its streets, and seeing a large polished halberd reared on each side of the doorway of a neat mansion, I was told they were there to indicate that the house was the residence of the Mayor for the time being, who happened then to be (as again in this year, 1877) Mr. J. Mitchell, the owner of extensive paper mills at Primrose, on the site of what were once noted print works, belonging to the Thompson family. And there is many another intelligent worthy there. Just and genial Wm. Smith—or dear James White! it would be hárd for me to pass the picturesque old borough and not think of them— the latter for his English, Irish, and foreign experiences; his books, his christian teachings, and our friendly conversations on rarest themes.

Giving a glance back towards the now spired village of Lowmoor, where the Garnetts, of Wadhow Hall, erected one of the earliest power-looms, from Clitheroe there is the choice of another pleasant route—partly an open field path—instead, (should you prefer it,) of going by Chatburn, to rustic and ancient little Worston (not Worsthorn), and thence, by shaded lanes and babbling brooks, to Downham—Pendle Hill looking impressively down, to the right, on your way. Downham Hall is the residence of R. Assheton, Esq., M.P. for Clitheroe, whose family has been distinguished in the neighbourhood from ancient days. The mansion, its grounds, and the proximate village, with the rich green vale just by, and Pendle looking down on the whole scene, Ingleborough and Pen-y-Ghent looming duskily but grandly in the distant sky, altogether make a more than ordinary attraction hither. If instead of coming by the fields you go to Chatburn by rail, it may be worth your while to

C

glance at the great limeworks in passing ; and as
the bed of limestone there is said to be altogether
thousands of feet thick, you need be under no appre-
hension of its early exhaustion.   Let me add that,
whatever there may be beneath, the air about
Clitheroe, Chatburn, Worston and Downham, is
the sweetest and healthiest you could wish to
breathe.

Bending round from Downham by Twisden,
and glancing at the fairy realm of Bowland while
doing so, we now come to what is popularly called
" the big end of Pendle," which, if you can climb
on that side, as many have done, you ought to be
at once enrolled an honorary member of the Alpine
Club, where for the present let me bid you a
kindly farewell.   Should the weather be fair you
could hardly find a lovelier view than that of
Bowland from this quarter.

CHAPTER IV.

GEOLOGY AND NATURAL HISTORY.

AS the semi-conical hill of Crich, on the carboniferous limestone, in Derbyshire, is noted for its strata, few degrees from the perpendicular, all leaning to the centre, as though there had been at some time a great internal convulsion and somewhat systematic upheaval; so with bulky Pendle Hill, though a ridge on the great Yoredale formation, its strata "lean to," much in the same way; and something akin to this may also be observed for some distance in the floor of Pendle Water at its feet. Dr. Whitaker says in reference to a great prehistoric catastrophe which must have affected the country north, south, and west of Clitheroe for more than forty miles, that "The crust of the earth appears to have undergone a violent disruption, in consequence of which the edges of the beds of the minerals were thrown up into the air and downwards towards the centre of the earth. At an angle of forty-five degrees immediately beyond this appearance arises the huge mass of Pendle, which seems to have been thrown up by the same convulsion; and to the north again appears a surface of limestone, with its concomitant system of plants and minerals, which, had the strata to the south maintained their natural [their first] position, must have lain at a vast depth beneath."

Between Pendle Hill and Downham is a minor eminence called Diamond Hill, and another between

Twiston and Downham called Ideson, in which are
found very beautiful crystals locally known by
the name of Downham diamonds.   Mr. William
Waddington, the Market-inspector of Burnley,
has a number of them in his possession—some so
pure and brilliant that it would take an adept to
distinguish them from the Golconda branch of
their family.

There must be something very antiseptic in the
earth near Pendle, or in its water (as I have also
seen in Ireland), since in Twiston Moss, oak, fir
and ash trees, with hazels amongst them that had
not yet cast their nuts, have been found, and which
must have been there for ages.

But among the most remarkable phenomena one
has ever heard of in connection with Pendle Hill
are the occasional bursts of water on its top or
from its bosom.   Camden mentions one of these
occurring in the year 1580 ; and Mr. Charles
Towneley, writing to Mr. Richard Towneley, in the
year 1669, describes " a mighty torrent" issuing
from the north-west end, on the 18th of August,
in that year, and says : " The water gushed out
near the top of the hill in such quantities, and so
suddenly, that it made a breast a yard high, and
continued running for about two hours.   It grew
unfordable in so short a space of time that it made
persons going to church on horseback, one having
passed the place where it took its course, the other
being a little behind, they could not pass this
sudden torrent.   The houses in the village of
Worston, at a distance of two miles from the
point of irruption, were so completely inundated
that the furniture in the lower rooms was set
afloat by the turbid stream.   Five or six apertures
[abrasures ?] were made in the side of the hill ;
but the longest of them was speedily closed by the
sand, earth, and gravel which accompanied the

Althorne Church.

Cawthorpe.

Towneley Hall

Mitton Church

water." So far Mr. Towneley, to whom we ought
to be thankful for his faithful record of the fact.
But it is a question with me as to whether or not
this "burst of water" was *on* the hill rather
than *from* it. During my own residence in Burnley
a far greater deluge came down by my house, in
Manchester Road, in the summer of 1870, ravaging
at the same time all the vale north of Holmes
Chapel and all the contrary vale to below Todmorden, as well as the vale of the Irwell on the
side of Backope. It made deep embrasures down
the sides of the Cliviger hills (I mean those on
the west side of the vale, for there was very little
of it on the east); it threw down, or nearly
gutted, several mills, displacing the machinery in
them with huge driven stones and mud. It
drowned two children and an old woman, washing
the latter away with the gable of the house she
dwelt in, between Rattenclough and Cornholme,
filling nearly all the other houses in that direction
with mud and stones; and was entirely over in
about two hours. It may probably take centuries
to obliterate its effects on the landscape for many
miles. In short, it was, only in infinitely greater
volume and force, just what Camden and Towneley
describe as occurring at Pendle. Two hours or
so from commencing the deluge had spent itself,
but the wreckage from it, which thousands came
from all parts of the country for several days to
see, was awful. I myself saw the dead body of
the poor woman who had been swept away with
her home, and she for pretty near quarter of a
mile had been carried down the Todmorden Road.
But all this was not owing to any *issue from the
earth* but to *the sudden liquification of abnormally
charged air on the hill-tops*. The sky was black as
night ere the water came down, near three o'clock
in the afternoon. Wherefore it is only natural

to consider if the phenomena at Pendle might
not have been of the same character, especially
as no great cavernous mouth or mouths remain
from which such bodies of water could have found
vent. There is record of similar phenomena
having occurred on Kinderscout, in Derbyshire,
and other mountains, in which one thinks elec-
tricity must have been a very active agent.

As regards zoology and botany the whole district is a most interesting one ; but as I have not
ascertained that it contains anything extraordinary to other parts of the country of a similar
cast, latitude and altitude, there will be no need
to dwell at length on the subject here. To the
angler it will be satisfactory to know that manufactures have not yet destroyed all the trout in the
streams. The ornithologist might enjoy himself
in searching for birds, and without much search
he may soon learn how crows and hawks abound,
while under the vigilance and voracity of the latter
the smaller quadrupeds and birds have become
rare ; that the wild plover, with its melancholy
" pe-weep," still sweeps over the ground ; while in
its season the cuckoo "from foreign parts " finds
the usual hospitable reception here ; and the lay of
the lark rings in the air as blithely as when echoed
in the sweet verses of Shelley, the Ettrick Shepherd, Samuel Bamford, or Richard Howitt ; and
that our old familiar friend, the water-wagtail is
by no means scarce among half-dried spots in the
bed of Pendlewater.

Although Pendle Forest does not equal old
Sherwood, Rockingham, or the New Forest, in trees,
it has many fine ones, and would, no doubt, have
had many more but for what in past times have
been used for building purposes as well as for fuel,
or for making clogs and bobbins. The under-
growth, however, is very rich and varied ; ferns of

many species are plentiful; and any rambler who loves to botanise by the way may have a perfect feast among the bonny herbs and flowers. I wish Henry Houlding, in such a beautiful book as few beside him could write, would come freely out and tell us all he knows about them.

The Forest has, however, produced a few extraordinary specimens of the *genus homo*. Here is an instance. One evening at the Crown Hotel, Colne, I happened to meet a Pendle forester who was a little sprung with drink, but still able to manipulate with tolerable nicety a tuft of unmanufactured cotton, for testing its degree of fineness, whereupon I asked him if he could test the cotton as precisely on being so far "gone" as in his normal state, when he at once kindly answered, "No!" Then, I asked again, what is the difference to your sensation; and how do you make allowance for it? "Why," he rejoined, "everything seems exaggerated, at least one-third, and I have always to make a proportionate deduction to obtain a right estimate." Well, I asked again, but does that rule apply as well to your estimate of yourself as to other matters? "That is so," he said, smilingly, "and I have to knock off in such circumstances a discount of at least thirty per cent. for that too, to get a right conclusion!" I wish every one under excited self-esteem could be as philosophical. Further acquaintance with the gentleman in question made me aware, that though a farmer by profession, and living in comparative isolation, he was well up in the poetry of Burns, Byron, and Shelley.

CHAPTER V.

BURNLEY: OLD AND NEW.

ONE of the principal as well as largest towns near to Pendle, undoubtedly, is Burnley. True, Colne may be more conspicuous on its own hill, and Gisborne on the other side more sylvan, rural, quaint, and, in itself, historically interesting, by the Ribble side. But as those places belong rather to a future work which I feel to be already growing in the mind, we may leave them, with many other loved scenes, for a time, and dwell awhile about the growing town on the Brun.

And I hear some persons affecting to regard manufactories and manufacturing towns as only disfigurements of a landscape; but come up with me some fine day, when the smoke is down, as far as bonny Spring Hill, or higher yet, to green Healey Height, and see. John Sutherland and the late Alderman T. T. Wilkinson, F.R.A.S., so well known as a mathematician and legendary writer, spent many a quiet hour there, feeling the vastness, beauty, and, I had almost said grandeur, of the prospect thence.

Little more than a generation since there lay a small country town of five or six thousand inhabitants down in that hollow, and few very conspicuous objects were there to mark it, save the old Parish Church-tower, the long, bright, right line of the Leeds and Liverpool Canal, that by its remarkably high embankment and aqueduct at what was then called Turf Moor, now Fulledge, seemed to span the town; while Bank House, in somewhat solitary dignity, looked back from its surrounding trees on all. The names popularly retained of some parts still tell the tale. Thorney Bank, Whin (the Gorsey) Hill, the Meadows, the Park, Pickup ·Croft, and Keighley Green, to say nothing of Healey Wood, Burnley Wood, and Burnley Lane, tell how the lark's trill, or the blackbird's, throstle's, cuckoo's, linnet's, and other " wood-notes wild," were heard there; and " Goodham Hill " reminds one of the descent there must have been from St. James's Street to the rivulet's grassy bank in that quarter, all now levelled over. The late Alderman Lord Massey (only just left us, at the age of nearly ninety-two) could well remember there being no bridge, but a shallow ford or stepping-stones in what is now Bridge-street; and worthy old Mr. Charles, at the Literary Institute, could give a hundred other particulars of that sort not less interesting. An old gentleman, James Sagar, ·only a few years since, pointed out to me from his garden-gate, at the foot of Spring-hill, the first little factory built in the town, which just now is incorporated with or obscured by larger erections, near Healey-wood; and thousands yet living could talk of the rustic games they played on ground since occupied by the principal urban streets and public buildings.

Yet look on what is now! The old Church-tower, the bright space of canal (said there to be the longest straight line of water between Liverpool and Leeds), and Bank Hall, though now populously surrounded, remain as I first saw them between thirty and forty years ago. Towneley Park, partly shorn of its trees and minus its scattered herds of fine deer, still retains a few of its patrician and forest-like features; and Boulsworth, the Mere-

clough Ridge, and Pendle Hill, yet form picturesque
back grounds as in the olden day; but all the rest,
how changed! Yon not ungraceful railway arches
to the north, the heavy unspired fabric of St. Marie's
to the east; Dr. Dean's rural residence of Healey
View, coming out as if to enjoy the sun and air in
the fields; the substantial and thriving Banks;
corn-mills, foundries, loom, cotton and iron works
of all kinds; the large Methodist, Baptist, and
other chapels in all directions; St. James's little
spire glinting up in the bottom of the town,
amid a forest of nearly two hundred long chim-
neys, yet looked down upon by Slater's most
useful clock-tower; and St. Andrew's spire, far
seen on Burnley Lane, now called Colne Road.
While instead of the old coach horns and songs
of birds, we hear loud railway whistles and
thundering trains, as they speed through the
massed homes of 50,000 people, whom shrewd
mathematical John Sagar says, if they go on
increasing at the present rate for 150 years, will
amount to more than *four millions!* Ah, friend
John, who can tell what may not happen to check
their progress ere then? One of the most remarkable things is the grand development of the late
Colonel Hargreaves's vast Coal-fields, with so little
disfigurement of either town or country, still going
on under more vigorous management than ever.

But whatever changes may have happened, the
old town does still cherish in its very heart a few
buildings not yet named that it would be wrong to
omit. The revered and beloved Canon Master,
formerly rector of Burnley, is gone; the present
rector, the Rev. Canon Townley Parker, M.A., resides
at Royle, the ancient and picturesque seat of his
family, about a mile off, where the Calder begins
to grow into a real river. But, "to what strange
uses may we come, Horatio!" Going up Parsonage Street, towards the Bank Top Station, or to

Royle, you see the venerable, many-gabled, mul-
lion-windowed old Rectory that gave the name to
the street, now the residence of a photographic
artist and site of his studio !

And then, on Keighley Green, which must in its
day have been a verdant little scene apart, with its
lawn and flowery frontage running down to the
rivulet's bank, may you not still see standing
what only a few years ago was the one Wesleyan
chapel of Burnley? Its exterior is little altered,
for Mr. Superintendent Alexander, with considerable taste, amidst all the factories around and their
smoke, has kept the place as neat and clean as
when it was half in the country ; but what a change
in its function! It was only a few evenings ago I
heard some one with more fun in him than
reverence, saying that it was "a house of prayer
turned into a den of thieves." True, it is now the
Borough Court-house, Police-office, and Lock-up
for felons ; but just look some day at the old
familiar spot, and think of its varied history. Many
an impressive sermon, many an eloquent lecture
has been given there, as well as many a prisoner
committed to the assizes or sessions. Even now, if
you go inside, you will see it in appearance almost
as much of a chapel as a " court-house" still. The
fine, dark-timbered old gallery remains the same ;
the pews below have been transformed to dock,
bar, and jury boxes, and the singing-seat into a
place appropriate to lawyers, clerks, and police
authorities. The pulpit has given way to the
magisterial bench. Yet the transition from chapel
to court has been so slight and brief that old
people who worshipped there in days gone by, some
times totter in to take a sort of pilgrim-peep and
" bless the Lord for the good they got there."
What was once the minister's residence adjoining,
is now that of Mr. Alexander and his family ; and

that gentleman, a native of the Land of Burns, connected by family-ties with the spot where the ploughman-bard wrote " Mary in Heaven," having himself a touch of poetry about him, and of kindly feeling, for which the world might hardly give an astute and alert police officer credit, though after many years of arduous service just now honourably retiring, has delighted, while adapting the place as well as possible to all present uses, to keep in mind and preserve the relics of its olden history. Note when you are there the newly brushed-up sun-dial on the front of the building, made with his own hand, and placed there by the Rev. P. Garrett, with the motto—" Boast not thyself of to-morrow, for thy sun may set this day nevermore to rise." It was a very beautiful and useful contrivance ; and when you turn to the green sward on which it looks, it may have the more effect if you be told, as I have some time been, that the body of the wife of the good and affectionate man who did it lies beneath, the only one there buried.

In the *Evangelical Magazine*, under date of Sept. 21st, 1814, the opening of Bethesda Chapel is thus recorded :—" A new chapel was opened for the public worship of God, at Burnley, in Lancashire. The Rev. Wm. Roby, of Manchester, preached from Psalm cxxxii. 17, 18 ; and the Rev. T. Raffles, of Liverpool, from Psalm xlviii. 3. It is right to say, that the friends of the Established Church have come forward, in a manner unprecedented, in aid of this infant cause. What a happy exemplification of that promise, ' and I will give them one heart.' " This is one of the events we may expect again, I believe, as our school-board contests vanish in the millenium. By the way, it is supposed that the minister first mentioned, was the father of Roby, the Lancashire historian.

No doubt many other curious and interesting

histories of places of worship and the vicissitudes
of their pastors might be written, were that our
object ; but I will confine myself to one, because it
comes more especially under my own recollection.
I wonder if this little work will ever reach the eye
of the Rev. John Reid, a native of Ayrshire, but
now labouring over the broad Atlantic. We happened once to dwell near each other in the English
Land of Lakes ; and it was our wont sometimes to
wander forth together there—he to see members
of his flock, and I to visit patients, among the
picturesque cloughs and fells, in whatever weather
might befal. I well remember one nobly-gifted,
but forlorn and lost inebriate he was the means of
converting, and who himself became for many years
one of the most loving and earnest recoverers
of others who had fallen, and a visitor of the
afflicted and bed-ridden, far and wide, until his
brain, probably owing to some effect of his earlier
habits, gave way, and he came to die at Marsden
Hall. Ah, poor, dear " Captain!" what a grand
intellect, and what a benevolent heart were thine
till that last constitutional sorrow ! On coming to
Burnley I found Mr. Reid also here, minister of
Salem Chapel, and residing up Manchester Road.
Here, as before, when duty would permit, we had
sometimes a pleasant stroll, for his health, especially after his Lake experiences, required it. But
that so failed him, and so many weakening cares
beset him, that at length he removed from Burnley
too. Let each one of us "speak of men as we find
them." I am sure it is the destiny of many to be
moved in the order of Providence for some good
and useful end from one place to another, like the
poor Frenchman in Dublin, who regretted " the
misforshune of having been born out of his native
land." And I trust Mr. Reid has found a true
home even on earth, if for nothing but his oft

kind criticism and encouragement of me. Should
this friendly thought ever reach his far Vancouver's
Island retreat, it may remind him of a few of our
pleasant walks together towards Buckclough and
Holme, as well as by Hesandforth (now Pheasantford, whither he was the first to guide me), and
to Briercliffe and far-seen and far-seeing Hag-gate,
where we enjoyed what God presented in nature
with thankful hearts and congenial aspirations.

But there are many lovers of nature, truth, and
poetry in and about Burnley, whatever its artificial
changes. I have certainly heard it spoken of as a
place fearfully smothered in its own smoke and
superstitiously given to idolising "brass" and tinsel.
Its population is, no doubt, kept down too by bad
nursing—by its cottage cradles being little better
than coffins on rockers, in which younglings are so
closely pent as to be incapable of moving their
tiny limbs, the custom being to rock the whole
body when they cry instead of giving natural
liberty to its parts ; and to promote bronchitis by
placing them half-way between the fire and an
open door in raw weather,—to say nothing of
choking them with tobacco smoke and other nasty
fumes; and it may take some time for Dr. Dean,
Alderman Coultate, Councillor Nutter, and all
the other sanitary genii, to convince everybody
of these and many other sins against sound
philosophy. But Burnley, unfortunately, is not
alone in these matters. And as to "brass," were
there no accumulators there could be no capital
for great works—were there no savers there could
be no helpers. None but the foolish ever rail
against wealth, if it be rightly used. And despite
a thousand things to regret, is there no tenderness
for the helpless—no concerted love of God and
nature and man, and of high duty, in the warm
and constant throb of those fifty thousand hearts

down there? If snobbery, impudence, humbug,
guile, mammon, and mutual distrust have here
and there temporarily superseded the old frank-
ness, unsuspecting good neighbourhood, natural
sense, and simple Christian piety, for which, as
some aged folks tell us, Burnley was once noted,
are true nobility of soul, bright intelligence, and a
kindly sincerity of purpose altogether gone? We
know better. Even though the woodland choir
and the sweet solos of throstle, linnet, or lark be
shut out, how many compensating organ tones,
family chords, and the swelling strains of social
and public concerts do we not hear? Christopher
Slater, thy labour, and that of many another good
musical leader, is not in vain! If old tales of
witchcraft are dying out—and let us hope that
drunkenness, street vulgarity, and social slander
will soon follow them—are not the various arts
and sciences all fast furnishing better topics? Is
not the religion of *warm Christian life* more valued
as *mere theological opinion* is losing ground; and is
there no hope of true political knowledge and
discrimination superseding blind party spirit
among thy growing sons and daughters, old
Burnley?

I said something of poetry; and are there no
poets here? Listen to Henry Houlding, and
wonder not that the Countess of Charlemont should
set such verse to music, when he writes on " Summer Days," and says :—

> " A little nook of wilderness
>   Between the meadow and the river,
> Where two erewhile together came,
>   And one will come no more for ever.
>
> The rustic bridge, the narrow road,
>   The seat upon the fallen pine,
> The whisper of the summer woods,
>   So sweet, but not so sweet as thine.

A little wild flower long ago
  Among the tangled grasses grew,—
So many things are dead since then,
  How should not we be withered too?

Here, where we sat, I sit alone,
  Watching until the sun goes down ;
For though 'tis summer time to-day,
  To-morrow will the woods be brown.

'Year after year,' the poet sang,
  Year after year the spirit sighs,
And summer days will come again,
  And suns will set in summer skies.

But to this bourne of wilderness,
  Between the meadow and the river,
Will any come because we came
  And say—They come no more for ever?"

Philip Gilbert Hamerton was born in or near
Burnley, and has said or sung—

          "Yes, I will earn
Success, fair Nature, in pursuit of thee ;
And to thy service thus I dedicate
All my bright future, sitting at thy feet.
I now can see, although I fail to grasp,
Thy purity within the waterfall,
And on the rippling surface everywhere,
Those living tints ascending from thy feet.
The trout do love thee, and the iris arch
Is thy tiara.   On the primrose beds,
And through the pendulous boughs, and round about
The banks of fern and hyacinth, and in
The hollows of the rocks, thy voice is heard
By those whose ears, undeafened by the roar
Of cities, can perceive thy melodies."

Hark, too, to Councillor Henry Nutter, as he
gaily sings on "Healey Height"—so near to his
own house—

"There's joy in the song of the lark as he rises,
  There's joy for his mate as she bathes in the dew;
There's joy for the boy with the girl that he prizes;
  There's joy in sweet friendship that ever proves true.

BURNLEY: OLD AND NEW.

Then sing, ye fair maids, in the valley before us,
  And shout, ye brave boys, your loud songs in the gale;
Ye sweet feathered songsters still join in the chorus,
  And chime, ye delightful old bells, through the vale."

Nor will my heart let me give the go-by to venerable and weary yet cheery old Mr. T. B. Spencer, who has more poetry in him than would suffice for a hundred ordinary rhymesters, and not a little good humour, would he but give them vent. Prosaic though it professed to be, what a flood of mental light did he not send forth in his recent paper on Spiritualism, at the " Literary and Scientific Club?" But probably there be many thinking bright thought in secret who would "blush to find it fame." Here is a touch of true *amor patriæ* from the people's playwright, Edward Slater, with which my too scanty extracts must now conclude :—

    " Some will sing of prouder places,
        Or the wondrous beauties tell
    Of far distant clans and races
        That 'neath fairer skies may dwell;
    But there's ne'er a clan or nation,
        Whatsoe'er be its renown,
    That I'd purchase with a furlong,
        Burnley! of thy dear-loved town."

And let us be thankful that if there be less breadth of wild moorland and depth of woodland to range near home, there is so much facility by rail and otherwise for getting afar, as the love of nature as well as of good fireside-reading intensifies; that there are still a few sweet and easy walks left for the aged and recreation grounds opening for the young; that art furnishes more food for taste as the wilderness narrows; and that we have still Healey Height, Mereclough Ridge, and grand old Pendle to ascend, if we will.

D

CHAPTER VI.

BURNLEY.—(CONTINUED.)

AND now turn out with me, on this "day so sweet, so calm, so bright, the bridal of the earth and sky"—the bridal also of May and June—and stroll with me through Towneley Park. Well-to-do families have many nice mansions overlooking it from the side of what was once Burnley Wood, and from Brunshaw; but we take the water-side, looking up now and then to the fine pastoral uplands leftwards, and on our right at antiquated Towneley Hall, with its somewhat sombre centre, its wings and towers, shaded by old ancestral trees; and yet, while itself half-hidden, looking out with a patrician air on its spreading domain, seeming to wear a smile of contentment with its own dignity and prospect,—a scene which "the Claimant" stated in evidence was *near Bath!*

There is something very remarkable in the history of the Towneley family, reckoning from before the Conquest, and in some of its members highly gifted with intelligence, patriotism, and fidelity. Faithful to its motto of "Tenez le vrai," and, one supposes, believing the latter to be in the Church of their fathers, they have continued Roman Catholics through the long ages, it is said, without a single break. As mentioned elsewhere, one of its sons was executed for his attachment to the Stuarts. But this is not the place for a detailed genealogy; and there is gloom within those walls just now, owing to the decease of Richard, only son of Colonel

TOWNELEY HALL.

John Towneley, the present representative of his
race.   I well remember the Colonel's father,
Peregrine—a shrewd, polite and intelligent gentleman of the old school, upon whose like we
may never look again.   I saw him once, when
John Sutherland and myself were having a stroll
by the then winding rivulet through the Park,
as Mr. Towneley, walked with a marvellously
elastic step down the road, till within our hearing,
and wishing to recall us to the track, politely
lifted his hat, and, almost stopping, bowed, saying
in a clear but not ungenial voice, "Gentlemen,
the grass will grow none the less if we keep the
road!" then marched on with the same spring-
step, while we took the hint and followed him.

When the late Lord Carlisle came to lay the
foundation-stone of the Burnley Mechanics' Institution, a large party of gentlemen met him
at Towneley Hall, at breakfast, and then formed
a procession from the hall to the town—the late
Col. Charles Towneley leading and presiding that
day.   Of course there were crowds of people in
the streets to see us pass—I say "us," having
been specially invited on that occasion to be there,
and to be one of the evening speakers.   On
nearing the aqueduct in Fulledge, Lord Carlisle,
with whom in the same carriage sat the late Sir
James Kay-Shuttleworth, broke into a laugh and
asked Sir James if he saw nothing remarkable
in the crowd they were passing.   Sir James, after
glancing round, "gave it up," when Lord C. said,
"Why, don't you see that every man and boy
of them has got his hands in his trousers
pockets?"   I remember its raining rather smartly
as, after a public luncheon, the stone was laid,
and that Salem Chapel, nearly opposite, was the
scene of the evening speech-meeting.   The last
time I saw Colonel Charles Towneley was at an

exhibition of poultry in the hall of the Institution
at the foundation of which he on that day officiated,
and which, as I ventured to recall it, he spoke
of with gratification.

And now let us take this upland path towards
Mereclough and Ormerod, glancing back and
around us often, as we go. How vast and varied
the scene, as we reach the high-road! Town,
mansion, park, fields, distant spire shooting up
like a rocket in the light, and dark Pendle in
all his majesty beyond. We also get nice glimpses of
the borough reservoirs, of Colonel Every-Clayton's
fair mansion of Rowley, Worsthorne (not Worston)
village, and of Ormerod House, thinking of the
name of Thursby, and then bend round to that
rare relic of Old England—Hurstwood. Ah! battle,
murder, and death may have done their work
around. Revolutions may over and over again
have shaken kingdoms. Trade may have many a
time changed for trade, and usurped the arena of
feudal life altogether. But here is a quiet village
of good-looking, substantial mansions, tasteful as
if they had, with their old gables, been arranged
exactly for sketching, as Philip Gilbert Hamerton
has sketched them with his skilful hand, and for
which all lovers of art and nature ought to feel his
debtors. Save one little Dissenting chapel, which
promises to grow grey in time, all here looks very
old, but very lovely; and with its bonny little
brooks and its neighbouring dells, Hurstwood is
undoubtedly one of the most interesting hamlets left
in England. It has been surmised, because some of
the ·residents here have borne the surname of
Spencer and the Christian name of Edmund, that
Edmund Spenser, the poet, himself once dwelt here,
and gathered the imagery of his " Shepherd's
Calender " from the dale below. If that and the
use of old English words be the only proof, the

hypothesis cannot be entirely relied on. I know a place near Wirksworth, in Derbyshire, where Spencers abound by the score, where the old language they use is almost identical, and where the scenery in the *Via Gellia* hard by answers to his descriptions quite as accurately. But nobody on these accounts ever sets up a claim for the poet as a resident there. Still, his name will hence be ever associated with this place.

Let us return by way of Worsthorne village; it is also a picturesque old place, and well worth seeing; then back, if not by Brunshaw, by Ormerod and Rowley, round each of which the scenery is very delightful, and down by Hesandforth (corrupted now-a-days to Pheasantford); and when we reach the venerable old Parish Church, the ancient inns, and relic of a cross hard by, we cannot, I think, but have arrived at the conclusion, that however Burnley itself may have grown into a town of industry and trade, its inhabitants have still ready access to some of the prettiest scenes of rural life in England, if they care for it. And though Burnley in itself may be full five days a week black and smoky enough—and it would be folly to deny that it must be so till manufacture has learnt to consume its own smoke—you cannot step or ride out of it in any direction without coming in contact with natural beauty and tasteful mansions dotting the scene.

For instance, what a quiet yet distinct and finely pronounced character has Ormerod! so sheltered yet elegant; in one sense of the word, so *select*; so beautiful and so winning withal! Don't trespass there, but get the reverend and urbane proprietor's leave to glance through, if you can and have a taste that way. Its plantations and lawns; its parterres and gardens; its architectural features including above all its two peculiar towers; and,

lastly, its relation to the fresh and ever refreshing
river, and its boweriness and floweriness altogether.
No words could accurately paint it, and the pencil
only in part.   It is *recherché* alike inside and out.
Its wonderful oak carvings within, so ancient in
their workmanship, yet so chaste and cheery in
effect; and the other articles of *vertu* it enshrines
in a retreat so sylvan: what a quiet, unpretentious,
yet dignified air pervades all!   I have to thank the
Rev. W. Thursby, M.A., and one of his gallant sons,
for courteously facilitating me in taking this men-
tograph of it the other day.   Up and down alike,
the Brun hence, murmuring its old yet ever new
song, has many interesting features, Hurstwood
being not far above; and the Hollins, now becoming
the residence of Mr. Charles Massey, as it was in
old time of the Hamertons, not far below.   There
are parts of Ormerod House, I believe, dating
from about the year 1100; yet it has many modern
features too, not at all discordant with them.

I have mentioned urbane Canon Parker's residence of Royle already, and other houses of similar
rank and antiquity.   But there is another order of
mansions which must certainly become ancient in
their turn, and which even now have something of
a patrician air and charm.   There is an irregular
chain of them extending nearly all the way to
Colne.   Long may it be ere Macauley's New
Zealander comes to sketch any of them!   They all
look towards Pendle Hill, and not only the Pendle
Water, but the Leeds and Liverpool Canal lights
up with bright and cheery glow the broad and
rich green vale between.   Again, the Brunshaw
and Todmorden Roads have many vying with each
other in taste.   There are also many, and more
still growing up in Manchester Road, (it would
be impossible to specify each,) to where Rose-
hill, Mr. Adam Dugdale's more imposing resi-

dence, looks back on them all. But we may loiter a moment at Spring-hill, the seat of kindly Miss Barnes, as it stands almost the first, commanding both town and country to a remarkable extent, and embracing what might not illogically be called a summary of the whole region. It would look directly down to the railway but for its own trees ; and has a fine view when the smoke is down of Pendle and Boulsworth, and all between, as well as of Towneley Old Deer Park, and is in itself a home of convenience and taste.

But a calm, bright Sunday, when the voice of labour is hushed and no mill smoke appears, is the time for seeing Burnley and its surroundings from the side of Manchester Road ; and a walk along it as far as the Clow Bridge reservoir at such a season, glancing down the vale of Whalley, and beyond at the distant hills, whether north or west, is a treat indeed, should the air be clear. There is now one house that way, a striking exception to most of the rest in being newly built of red brick—the residence of Mr. Duckett. It is not at all out of keeping with taste, and should it stand the weather as well as one hopes, it will lose none of its dignity when touched by age.

The road towards Accrington, too, opens up some fine views, including one of the Hambledon Hills and another of Padiham, the spire of Habergham, and several superior mansions in that quarter, with Pendle Hill beyond. Turning to the left near to the gate of Holme Lodge, now the residence of Mr. Henry Lomas, and late of Mr. Richard Shaw, who was the first Member of Parliament for Burnley, we soon arrive at the CEMETERY —a scene worth visiting for more than being a repository of mortality. Of its chapels I will say nothing, except that they are comfortless places for the poor mourners and ministers who have to use them; but of the scenes around it would be difficult to say too much in praise.   The gracefully descending slopes, the wooded and streamy clough at the bottom, the pastured and cultured fields, the sunbright water-gleams and surrounding hills, all combine, with the solemn use of the place, its monuments and many touching associations to make Burnley Cemetery remembered with tenderness and "joy in grief" by all who may have occasion to visit it.   In such a scene of "storied urns and animated busts," it would seem rather invidious, perhaps, to specify any.   Yet there are a few good striking monuments, including that to Healey, the musician, well worth attention, and a few spots where I saw the sleeping ones laid that will ever have a tender interest for me. Dear, ready-witted, kind-hearted, genuine, devoted Willie Gill—a very Kirke White in the sacrifice of body to soul; like him, too, early taken, and by an ailment of the same organs; but without a Southey to make thee famous—I saw thee laid here!   And she, dear old Mrs. Lord Massey, ripe in goodness as in years, the mother of all the poor, the bereft, the suffering in any way, around yonder mansion overlooking the fall of Pendle Water— her lately laid nonegarian partner by her side! The memory of her and her examples of love and duty ought never to die.   Wave gently ye leaves, and bloom sweetly ye flowers, over those graves!

But what shall I say of rare JOHN SUTHERLAND, my friend in council, the critic of half my writings, sympathiser in all my vicissitudes, for more than thirty years?   I doubt much if Burnley ever had a brighter brain or warmer heart than his; but while thinking for others he allowed himself too little rest.   He literally let the Post-office, of which he was master, kill him; for whatever the weather of early morning or late evening he would come and

go, and appropriated too little of life's comforts
in the hours between, so added exhaustion to
exhaustion, cold to cold, and died of complicated
pleurisy and pneumonia on the 23rd of December,
1873. All parties felt the shock when he fell, and
after the fall some stir was made about raising a
public monument to his worth. About seventy
pounds was subscribed. An old mutual friend
nominated me on the committee for it, and I
attended one meeting to hear it decided without a
single murmur, save my own, that the monolith to
be purchased with the money should not have anything on it to *describe the man*, but simply to tell
the naked facts of his age, the time of his death,
and that he was postmaster of Burnley—as any
other good man without one tithe of his genius
and intellectual qualities might have been—for a
stated number of years. There stands the all but
barren stone. But, "because he needs no praise,
shall I be dumb?" Let me here venture to record
what was spontaneously shed by my own poor pen
on the day of his funeral. It is no disparagement
of the present most excellent and assiduous postmaster, Mr. Garrett, to speak thus warmly of his
predecessor:—

JOHN SUTHERLAND.

There is a blank in Burnley town to-day,
  Which ev'n the landscape round it seems to know;
And as his manly corpse is borne away
  Our hearts feel fuller for the general woe.

A warrior brave was he on duty's field,
  Where, hero of a bloodless fight, he fell;
Not in the harshest weather would he yield—
  True to the onerous post he fill'd so well.

The early thrush's note from Springhill went
  With him, to cheer him in thy morning, May!
And down the far-off lark from Healey sent,
  To catch his wistful ear, its kindred lay.

And much he loved the notes of each glad singer,
  For Nature's harmonies to him were sweet,
Yet not another moment would he linger
  When work required him down the unwaken'd street.

Still, though in spring or summer he denied
  Himself communion with her in her beauty,
He shunned her not when, with fierce storms allied,
  She smote his bosom on the path of duty.

For oft in winter's morning—rain, or sleet,
  Ere yet his chill from yesterday was o'er—
Ere yet the mill-clogs clattered through the street—
  His solitary step came by our door.

And then a storm of letters on his ken
  Broke in from north, and south, and east, and west,
With order due to be dispatch'd again,
  Yet even that achieved gain'd him small rest.

    *   *   *   *   *   *

Dear SUTHERLAND! oh, never more shall we
  Have one thy functions better to perform,—
Oh, never more in any office see
  A man more firm, yet patient, kind, and warm!

With grace for grace thou could'st the loftiest meet,
  With kindliest smile the lowliest comer serve,
The sad and sore with consolation greet,
  Yet ne'er from discipline or order swerve.

Oh, who can tell what Burnley owes to thee,
  Thy manful, yet unostentatious life,
Thy love for individual liberty,
  Thy hatred strong of all malignant strife?

Oh, who can tell how many a far-off land
  Has knowledge of thy bright benignant eye,—
Thy cheering words discreet, and generous hand,—
  For every wanderer had thy sympathy!

    *   *   *   *   *   *

But cease this strain, for thy reward is great;
  In a still nobler life thy faith was strong;
Thy intellect, while here if bright and great,
  Will brighter be amid the angel-throng!

We lay thy body in its grave to-day,
  Thy oft-climb'd uplands grandly looking down,
And pensively return upon our way,
  No more to meet thee in the pulsing town.

But when the thrush to Springhill comes again,
   And sings the lark o'er Healey in its glee,
Or winter's blast drives harsh the chilling rain,
   We'll often think, dear John, of thine and thee.

December 27th, 1873.

It ought to have been told on the memorial-stone
that few men in his day had unostentatiously done
more for the intellectual and social improvement
of his native town.

As yet, having heard nothing of any intended
public monument to the late Alderman T. T. Wilkinson, though there was much demonstration at his
funeral, I take it for granted that he is supposed to
have left a sufficient memorial of himself in his
literary works.

In a quaint book before me, by Stephen Rey-
nolds Clarke, published in 1830, I now read :—
" Burnley, a market town and chapelry in the
parish of Whalley, hundred of Blackburn ; 9 miles
S.E. of Clitheroe, 211 from London.   Inhabitants,
6,378."   This, of course, did not include Habergham Eaves, which had then about two-thirds of
the same number.   The same writer speaks of a
cross near the Church of great antiquity ; and
also says, there are " three meeting-houses for
Dissenters and a Catholic chapel," adding other
topographical particulars not needful here.

CHAPTER VII.

Ightenhill (or Hightonhill) Park.

ORLD within world, realm within realm, rare little epitome of feudal and rural Old England! What a treat to run out for an hour's poetic or artistic revel in thee! A short mile's walk from Burnley, nearly as far as the "Tim Bobbin," on the Padiham Road, then a turn into a side lane on the right, and from it a gentle bend round to the left, a few steps along a public way—too public to be called a mere "occupation-road," too private to be regarded as one for all sorts of vehicles—and you soon come to a primitive-looking farmhouse, built by the grandfather of Mr. James Smith, the present occupant, from the last relics of Ightenhill (anciently, Hightenhull) Hall, or Castle, close by,—in its day one of the most important manorial mansions in the county; but now reduced or restored (choose which word you best like) to the plainest and greenest pasture, its site commanding some of the finest views of woodland, field, and mountain that eye could desire. And I believe there can be no question as to John of Gaunt, Duke of Lancaster, and other persons of historic note, having once resided here.

Down below, after receiving Pendle Water,

winds the West Calder. Asserting itself above its
surrounding plantations, rises the tower of Gawthorpe Hall, to the left, with the town of Padiham
and fells and slopes of Whalley beyond. Straight
before you to the north, somewhat centrally, bask
white Hunterholm and grey Pendle Hall—the
former conspicuously, the latter only just seen.
To the right swells up the country eastward, embracing the brisk young townlets of Brierfield and
Nelson, to Caster Cliff, or Tum-hill, the site of a
Roman or other ancient encampment, near Colne ;
while wide and far upward before you stretches a
green pastoral space, interlineated here and there
by some picturesque clough or coppice-wood, with
gathered herds or scattered flocks between ; and
Pendle Hill in the back ground—grand monarch of
all—dimly blue, or green, or variously streaked,
according to the prevailing light and the season.
What a glorious arena ! gaze till you have taken
it all in ; then turn down one of the footpaths a
little backward to the right, soon passing a small
hamlet, and descending one of the most primitive
and pretty old English lanes to the " Pendle
Hipping-stones," cheered by the minstrelsy of
wood-birds and the blended breathings of wild
flowers, from those of the " milk-white thorn " to
the wild thyme, cowslip, and honied clover.
Heavens, how delicious all ! And as you pass
along, note well the groups of various trees and
green holly bushes that make you feel as far from
the stir and smoke of the town as you could have
expected to be in a hundred miles' ride. Wander
wherever you may in this quarter, you cannot get
out of the unmistakeable atmosphere of loveliest
Nature, nor long out of the sight of fairest land-
scapes, or sound of sweet voices.

And now you are down at the lower " Hipping-
stones," different from, however like to, those

near which the Burnley sewage finds vent towards
Danes House. Mind how you tread them; or, if
you be weak or timid, don't risk the experiment.
Should the current of the river be, as it often is
here, somewhat deep and strong, turn back by the
way you came, or by any other you can find, for
you will meet with beauty everywhere while returning. But if you be elastic, strong and brave, spring
across from stone to stone, and climb to that
remarkable green mound, " crowned with a peculiar diadem of trees in circular array, so fixed, not
by the sport of nature, but of man," popularly
known as " Seven Trees," the eyrie of a venerable
rookery, and close neighbour to antique Pendle Hall.
The trees, I have heard, were planted as a family
memorial by some ancient denizens of the Hall.

What that mound, partly natural and partly
artificial, may have been used for in the olden
day, nobody residing near may now be able to tell
you, nor can they tell you much, save that in their
judgment " it always was so," about the picturesque old mansion, degenerated in the progress
of other things into a farmhouse, on an estate of
Major Le Gendre Starkie, of Huntroyd, by its side;
but the whole scene, with the white house of
Hunterholm observed from Ightenhill, near by,
will more than repay our visit; and we can come
away by the river-side to the upper "Hipping-
stones," and so back to Burnley by Royle, or by
Danes House, Bank Hall, and the New Grammar
School. But before entirely quitting the scene, let
us turn and gaze on the sky above it; for in the
language of my gifted friend James Hurnard,*

" Sweet is the close of the young summer's day,
 Sweet as the heavenly smile of dying saints;

---

* Author of that most remarkable poem, " The Setting Sun,"
which ought to be better known, being not so entitled from any
exclusive relation to sunset and its attendant phenomena, but
because it is written in the sunset of his life, and reflects all his
interesting experiences, observations and philosophies.

The air is calm, the very clouds repose;
The beamy sun sinks peacefully to rest.

   *   *   *   *   *   *

The prism of the horizontal air .
Subtends the red rays of the setting orb
Upon a panorama of rich clouds,
Whose gorgeousness is the despair of art.
The western sky is like an emerald sea
With golden islands floating on its bosom,
Islands of purest transcendental joy,
Peopled with happy angels in bright robes;
But while we gaze entranced the pageant fades."

CHAPTER VIII.

Cliviger Vale.

ONE of the most romantic little valleys in the North of England is the Vale of Cliviger—a craggy, wooded, and streamy cleft through the pastoral hills between Burnley and Todmorden—formerly about as lonely and retired as it was rugged, but now growing populous, and so threaded, not only by a good Macadamised road, but by the railway, as to be easily reachable in every part, even by little children. If going on foot, it will be best, perhaps, to start through Towneley Park, but if by rail, from the Manchester Road Station. By either method it is only about nine miles through, and as you go along keep a wakeful eye on each side; for besides the charms of wood and pasture there are, especially after rain, a few pretty water-falls to cheer you.

On getting about two miles from Burnley, past the celebrated Towneley Coal, Coke, and Drain-pipe Works, on looking up to the right you see a lofty swell of country culminating in a one-cotted neighbour to the sky, called Crown-point. Further on in that direction is a hill, now called Thieveley, which I take to be a contraction and corruption of Th' Heigh Lea (*i. e.*, The High Lea). Beneath Crown-point winds a road towards Back-ope, corrupted into Bacup, across Deepley, contracted into Depley, then corrupted into Derpley—writers who bury their eyes in books, forgetting simple nature and common sense, and accounting for one name by a notion that the deer of Rossendale *backed up* there, and for the other, that they went to its pastures to *play*. Such logic is about equal to that of the man who said in reference to Mesmerism, notwithstanding the name of Mesmer who used it, that it was so called because those who meddled with it generally got into a *mess*. Deepley, contra-distinct from Highley in position, as it is, would be commonsensical and descriptive; and as to Back-ope, not only was it long ago so spelt, but any one on that side may see that it is a *back opening* from broad Rossendale. Those who know the north of England and south of Scotland are well aware that such places are commonly called *opes* or *hopes*. Thus we have Tunstalhope and Ryehope in Durham, Hopetoun in Scotland, Hope village and Hopton in Derbyshire, and probably a hundred other such instances, were it worth while, might be quoted in relation to similar localities. If you are at any time on foot, and have strength and leisure, make a detour to Thievely or Deepley, or both: the views would well repay the toil. You might come back by Buckclough, which Mr. Carswell, formerly superintendent of the county constabulary at Burnley, has with true Scottish tact and perseverance, in a wonderfully short time changed from a comparative desert into one of the best of farms; and bonny is the beck that babbles by his door, as if to thank him.

But we are not going up thither just now. Let us imagine ourselves arrived at Holme, or Holmes Chapel, as it is more generally called—perhaps to distinguish it from other places of the same name. We have passed Barcroft Hall and some water-mills on our left; have mated again with the "ribble-bibbling" Calder as we came along; have

E

noticed the high pastoral uplands scaling the sky there, and are now on classic ground.

In this antiquated mansion with its low retiring centre, its two projectant wings, and its quaint mullioned windows, dwelt and wrote the late Dr. Whitaker, historian. It was he, too, who planted most, if not all, of these grand woods, now so mature, for which in their younger growth he had awarded to him a national premium. Some of them seem to be climbing from and some to be descending and bowing to the old mansion, which is now owned by a gentleman of his own race and name—a leading county magistrate—while his ashes are laid amid the scene of his literary and arboricultural labours, in or near the neat Italian-looking chapel hard by.

And the mortal remains are also laid there of one whose name is a household word, not only in these regions, but throughout the empire—the late General the Hon. Sir James Yorke Scarlett. For myself, I do not love war. In its aggressive character it is horrible. But all men admire bravery and self-devotion in any cause. General Scarlett had both the latter; and his hair was growing silvery ere he led " the celebrated charge at Balaclava," with which his name is always now connected in the British mind.

One day I saw the veteran's manly person on horseback in Burnley street, and a few evenings afterwards marked the ease, dignity, and *bon homie* with which he sat as chairman in the hall of the Literary Institute, while Mr. W. Farrer Ecroyd was addressing a body of Conservatives there; but not many more days had passed, when death, with but little warning, smote him down, not in the field where its dart had so often missed him in the thick fight, but in his quiet residence, Bank Hall, where it looks down on the murmuring Brun, in the midst of old attached neighbours and friends. I saw the mournful cortege as it passed throngh Towneley Park hither on the day of his funeral— the gun-carriage that bore his coffin preceded and followed by a line of carriages that stretched almost across the park and into the crowded road beyond it. The rain poured copiously, and the people poured down too, to line the melancholy vale that day ; and I should think that good old Mr. Sutcliffe, the parish clergyman, could hardly have fore-imagined the surging throngs that thus peopled the scene of his usual quiet labours. Bank Hall stands much as it did, the elegant newly-built Grammar School near; the two great guns from the Crimea, given through the General as keepsakes, hold their places by the road, at Brownhill; and in the town people yet talk of him almost as if he were still amongst them ; while railway passengers, as the train flits past Holme, point from the windows, and say, " Dr. Whitaker, the historian, and General Scarlett, are buried *there.*"

A few more steps, or a few minutes' ride by rail, passing some beautifully shaded pools, the resort of shy waterfowl, by the way, and we come to " the Summit," at the source of two streams— twins by birth, but taking contrary ways, one the West and the other the East Calder—Calder being the name by which many other streams in the neighbourhood are called, and each of these two growing anon to a considerable river.

From this point the glen grows more ample, rocky, and watery as we proceed, though more and more populous as we reach signs of manufacturing enterprise—the variegated woods, the emerald meadows, the projecting crags, and the distant blue hills forming altogether a picture at once beautiful and sublime, and justifying the name of *Tor-mer-*

den, still so pronounced by the descendants of the
old natives ; but some time or other corrupted by
the pen, perhaps, when semi-dunces from Nor-
mandy had to write it, to *Todmorden*. Tor-mer-
den was simply a beautiful and accurate descriptive
name for a dale of tors (rocks) and waters. As
for this grand scene ever getting its name from the
tod (fox) on a moor and hens in the valley, as the
book-fellows say—that is about as babyish as their
derivations of Bacup and Derpley. James Standing, author of " Echoes from a Lancashire Vale,"
who was born here, or other writer, may some day,
perhaps, tell a far better tale.

Another word or two about the waterfalls. The
chief of them is at Rattenclough, a little way on
the Burnley side of what has been—unfortunately,
I think—named Portsmouth. There is another at
the back of Messrs. Collinge's Cliviger Mills, and
several further on. Sometimes, it is true, there
may be scarcely more than a tinkling rill down any
of them ; but after a copious shower, or a night's
steady rain, down comes a deluge, roaring and
foaming—a little Niagara. I have already told
the story of one flood breaking over the neighbouring hill-tops in the summer of 1870, drowning
people, and throwing mills, houses, bridges, and
works of all sorts into complete wreckage. But
how sunny and calm on this pleasant spring day !
What a lovely scene is over-looked by yon lofty
chapel of Shore ! How neat, but modest, stand this
little Baptist fold and friendly pastor Chapman's
house by the road below ! How projects that high
" Eagle Crag," naturally configured like the large
bird lending it a name, and seeming ready to swoop
down on the distance-dwarfed people plying at
their doors beneath ; and freshly and deliciously
spread the meadows, winds the river, and rise the
mansions as we near Todmorden town. Ah, well-

remembered old John Fielden! I do not wonder at this generation feeling proud to raise memorials of thee there. But to go much further in that direction would be trespassing on a region which I may some day have to take for the theme of another book. One more little anecdote from my own experience shall, therefore, close the present story.

In the month of December, 1869, the illness of a professional friend called me almost daily from Burnley to Rochdale. One evening I was up at a lofty place called Summer Castle, in the latter town, after the streets had been lit, but before the shops and factories had been closed, so that far and thickly spread the lights glowing like stars in a nether sky. On reaching Todmorden, when returning, the gas-constellations studding the picturesquely-formed hills and dales in every direction there were still more striking and curious. Moonlight slept in the vale as our train came along by Holme; and on reaching Towneley Station the windows of all the factories in and near Burnleywood were still a-glow, the clear moon over Towneley, now near its full, calmly presiding over all the lights. It was a glorious evening, for the smoke had nearly gone down, and the stars above were brightly twinkling.

Next day—it was Christmas Day—the world around seemed all crisp and clear, just a little frosty, as though it were early spring rather than winter, the ivy and bright evergreens of all sorts favouring that pleasant illusion. At Todmorden Station I had long to stay between the arrival of one train and departure of another, listening to the strains of an excellent brass band that was playing sacred melodies through the town—the factories all still, and the castled and cotted heights seeming like myself to be listening, as no doubt the good people in them were.

The day following that was Sunday; but as I
went again, how changed was all the scene! A
wuthering and *swithering* snowstorm was driving
through the vale with a force that nothing less
energetic than a railway-engine could have met—
no Barcroft, no Bucclough, no Holmes Chapel, no
Rattenclough, or Eagle Crag, no anything to be
seen through the clouds of feathers, driven so
thickly that they seemed to lack their natural
whiteness.

The day following that, how changed again! The
air was as calm and clear as if there had never
been a storm in the world. The pure virgin snow
lay in fleeces, wreaths, and light flosses on all the
ground, the rocks, and trees ; a mantle of hoar-
frost had added its pure and solemn charm ; and
thus in four consecutive days I had seen the whole
vale in almost every aspect of the four seasons.

Heptonstall (which a travelled gentleman once
told me presented, with its surroundings, an excellent miniature resemblance of Jerusalem), the
grand scenery about Mytholm and the Lumb,
Hebden Bridge and Hardcastle Crags, might all
be reached in a single day, commencing with what
I have here attempted to outline of Cliviger Vale;
and the whole of England could hardly afford a
more pleasant day's " outing " for a good pedes-
trian, were he artist, naturalist, geologist, zoologist,
poet, or altogether.

CHAPTER IX.

Glimpses of the Brun, or Burn.

IN no part of the country—not even in Derbyshire or the region round about Sheffield—are there "cloughs," "greaves," "denes," "burns," "grips," "dumbles," or "glens," as they are variously called in various places, more retired and romantic than some round Burnley. And in seeking them out we sometimes get among scenes that *feel* as remote from modern stir—as ancient, pastoral, and solemn—as if they were in Syria or Circassia. They are so near to nature, yet so associated with human history and interests; and you also find your way to them through so much that is antique and picturesque— some old decayed farmstead, or shattered cottage at least, in view—as to feel while gazing on them taken back a thousand years. Whenever there, one experiences an ecstatic yet aching sort of wish that it were possible to bring them away to the fireside. Philip Gilbert Hamerton has almost done this in a part of his exquisite little volume, "The Isles of Loch Awe and other Poems,"—in a pencil-sketch in rocky "Water-gate," near Hurstwood, vignette to "A Dream of Nature;" and I wish it were in my power to imitate him further up the stream, and in the tributary dale of Shedden, or Shedding, to which we will now try to find our way—say from Burnley.

If you are not strong, start with any procurable conveyance up Brunshaw Road as far as Fox-stones, taking an occasional survey of the town behind and the outspread country on either side as you proceed. Beyond Fox-stones a carriage can little help you. But if you are hale and elastic, get your walking-stick, and stroll away by Hesand-forth, Rowley, and Ormerod, or through Towneley Park, then up by Mereclough and along the old Roman "Causeway" till you come to the now dilapidated "Pot Ovens;" then turn to the left through a gate leading to the Pastures. There are three farms of the latter name. I daresay farmer Harrison, who occupies the first, or his wife, will be pleased to direct you forward, if you are courteous and kind, and, possibly will sell you a refreshing draught of milk as well, should you require one. Or better still, perhaps, turn up a little short of Mereclough to Fox-stones, where old Mrs. Crowther, or some other good body, may be able to tell you the exact whereabouts of what you are seeking, for she has all her life dwelt there. Or if you have come up by Brunshaw-road to Ormerod-gate, you can make for Hurstwood (at all times so well worth seeing), and inquire there. Anyhow, you cannot easily get wrong if you take any of the courses named, and ask the way down to the Hipping-stones, near Rock-cottage. Here you will find yourself in company with the Brun or Burn, four miles above the town to which it lends its name ; and it will much depend on the season and the weather as to the terms you will have to keep with it. If the water coming down be about its average quantity and force, you may soon, with a little contrivance, find yourself in Hamerton's favourite nook, among picturesque bits of rock; naked, twisted, and crinkled roots and boughs, mosses, ferns, flowers, miniature waterfalls (in Scotland called *lins*), and flickerings of sunshine and shadow playing at hide-and-seek ;

while a hundred birds may, if in spring or early summer, be adding their music to that of the rollicking, revelling, trout-haunted stream,—a " little heaven below " for the naturalist, artist, or lover of the country, of whatever tribe or school. I believe that Mr. Jerry Smith, (as he is familiarly called in Burnley,) may be seen seeking herbs there nearly every week, three parts of the year.

Much the same may be said of the dell as it strikes its upward way for about quarter of a mile; and whoever explores it must be guarded against accident, for in places its rocky sides are very steep and the water deep.

Further on, the ravine becomes more open and divided—Cant Clough, the main source of the Brun, bending a little to the left as you ascend it, and Shedden, or Shedding, to the right. If Shed'n (as the people pronounce it, imagining, like the old Derbyshire postman, perhaps, that it " never needs spelling ") is so called from being meadowy, it should manifestly be spelt with the terminal *ing*; if simply from its being a natural hollow, *den*. But on coming fairly in sight of it you will be too startled for mere etymological speculation.   Stretching, and widening as it stretches up, into the bosom of a mountain moor, it abounds, as you will see, with the most extraordinary hills and hillocks of dark-grey stones, weeded out and precipitated, after being disintegrated and washed as useless from the limestone got by an ancestral people so long ago, that all which now remains of their work here looks as wild, hoary, and forgotten, as though it were antediluvian! Heaps as large as the " groove-hillocks " in the Peak country, and in Cornwall, Northumberland, or Wales; and others so small, they might have been drifted by a mere wavelet of Morecambe Bay, or the curvetting sea that plays with pebbles on the shore at Brighton; but all, where not quite naked and smooth, "mossed and lichened over," or giving shelter to the larkspur or some other delicate flower as it peeps up into the light, and interspered with blooming haw-thorns, delighting the vision and filling the air with fragrance, as I and my neighbour, Richard Nelson, recently saw them on a warm day in June.

But that is not all. Come up hither out of the deep obscure on to this pasture spreading to the south-west, while commanding the northern and western view, and look abroad. See, on the right, how finely the zig-zagged and streamy clough ends in wood, furze, and fern; how pleasantly Shedden Farm basks in the opposite fields; how pic-turesquely yon ancient stone-quarries are scarring and ribbing the hillsides; how umbrageously the Ormerod plantations mantle on the eye, beyond those grey old gables of Hurstwood hamlet; how, far away to the north, as Boulsworth and chapel-crowned Hag-gate are swelling up rather nigh, the tops of Whernside, Ingleborough, Pen-y-Ghent, and other Yorkshire heights, just catch the sight; while calm, dark, and almost sublime, king Pendle tells us how hard it would be in all the scene to find a spot whence he may not be beheld. Nor is this to be wondered at, considering how you may some-times see York Minster, so it is said, from his summit, or he may himself be seen from the neigh-bour of Harrogate. But I doubt if there be a finer view of him anywhere than from our present position. And as you leave it on your return, I doubt also if you could anywhere better than from a point between Ormerod and Mereclough obtain views of Burnley town, Towneley Hall and Park, and the western woodlands, fields, and far-off moors, or of the plantations down towards Holmes Chapel, in Cliviger Vale.

But, if instead of returning that way, you should bend aside, as is possible, towards Worsthorne, you will get glimpses of the Burnley Water-work reservoirs, about Swinden—forming a bright foil to the dusky moors and green fields around. And not far from one of these, besides Worsthorne village you will see some outlying rural home-steads—one occupied by Mr. Bellingham and his family, which I can never see without thinking of his history. But for the lapse of title, through one of his near ancestors having been abroad and the family too long omitting their claim, Mr. Belling-ham, instead of occupying that humble cottage and so diligently superintending his well-known shop at Burnley, might have been at this hour lord of the distinguished halls of Levens and Cunswick, in Westmoreland, and all their choice domains! Having once lived near them, and been accustomed to hearing the matter talked of by people well-informed, I know that this is true. One of his ancient ancestors was Viceroy in Ire-land, doing most good and signal service there. An effigy of that knightly person, or some other of his race, is distinguished in Kendal parish church; and were our townsman, so unaffected, yet gentlemanly as he is both by birth and character, to be recognised in Kendal streets, there is hardly a person there who would not respectfully acknowledge him, in such reputation is the name he bears still held; and I do not think it dishonoured by being in Mr. William Bellingham associated with honest trade. But I am digressing, yet not without a hope in this instance of being forgiven.

Winding round between Hurstwood and the sylvan pleasaunces of Ormerod, down by Rowley and Hesandforth, the Brun receives several other feeders, a few of them at their junctions with it furnishing capital points for good sketching—St.

Andrew's spire in the mid-view and Pendle Hill
in the back-ground being from several places well
seen; while its stream many a time makes one
think of that expressive stanza in John Edwards's
"Tour of the Dove:"—

"Thou eldest of the elements, which sprang
From underneath the Spirit's brooding wings,
When chaos heard that potent voice which rang,
Commanding life and being to all things:
Hail, water! Beautiful thy gushing springs,
Thy lakes and rivers! Shrined in clouds or dew,
In ice or snow, or where the rainbow flings
Its radiant arch, in every form and hue,
Thou, glorious element! art ever fair and new."

CHAPTER X.

BRIERFIELD AND NELSON.

UNTIL scenes still rapidly changing have become "stereotyped," it can be of little use to describe them except in a cursory way. Great and Little Marsden, aforetime so called! What were they only one generation since? Imagine yourself on a stroll along "Marsden Heights" but a few years ago, and looking north, east, or west,—Brierfield a briery wilderness, as its name implies; Nelson, a solitary inn for calling travellers, or at most a farm or two; a small hamlet here and there, and a few wide-apart places of worship, including St. John's church and the venerable though plain Friends' chapel, silent as the gathered dead (now including brave and worthy old William Ecroyd,) in its green and shaded little enclosure; Lomeshaye works just beginning to develope by the gleaming river's side; here a patrician mansion, and yonder a tall farm-house, not much unlike a Scottish or Northumbrian peel; and the whole pastoral vale, a large cradle waiting for the railway and the baby towns,—the latter already growing into giants, with their local boards, gas-works, large mansions, larger factories, and rising churches, as we see them! This last, bent, stiff-knee'd vestige of the ancient population, in his old round hat, corduroy breeks, smock-frock, and greasy fustian gaiters, a short pipe in his mouth, and spade or pick-axe over his

shoulder is just the man to tell you all about it.
When he was a shepherd-boy on Marsden Heights,
and then a quarryman,—on the Leeds and Liverpool Canal (not long made,) so nearly parallel with
Pendle-water, there stood by the side of the new
road from Burnley to Colne a single public-house
called the " Nelson Inn." Presently, as factories
began to rise, cottages and shops began to cluster
and then expand around it—all taking their name
from that one public-house; and thus it was the
town of Nelson grew—Brierfield rising much in
the same fashion, but retaining its old wild name,
the only uncivilised feature now left about it being
the Lancashire and Yorkshire Railway-station,
where often from fifty to a hundred people, or
more, are waiting for a train, with inadequate
shelter from the rain ; and (though the Directors
have been *for years* appealed to on the subject)
there is only one place d' convenience, about as
narrow and handsome as a pig-stye, *for both sexes,*
and where I have beheld scenes it would be im-
proper to sully this page by describing,—enough,
after what the Hon. Justice Denman said about
local barbarism on trying that fearful Mereclough
case, to make his lordship tear off his wig and
ermine in rage, if told that this kind of education
is sanctioned by a body of non-resident directors
—the members of which may be genteelly enjoying themselves in clean and distant mansions.
Thank Heaven, however, that this is a great
exception to the tone of the neighbourhood in
which it is permitted, and which, one naturally
thinks, cannot much longer brook such an insult
to common decency!

If we pass from Burnley to Colne by rail, there
is much worth seeing of rural beauty—*rus in urbe*
—here and there, as well as much of mineral and
manufacturing industry. In such a number of

pleasant residences as mark the scene, since it is impossible to specify all, it would seem invidious to dwell on any, here. Yet it is hard to pass some of them without a genial word. From smiling Reedley Lodge, and Reedley Hall, to bonny Heirs House, just beyond Colne Railway-station, with its lawns and magnificent views, and the glorious command of watered vale, rising pastures, and the Pendle Forest back-ground seen from them all, as I have hinted before, what a continued chain there is of elegant if not all stately homes!

Or if instead of taking the rail we go by the old or new Colne road, how much there is to arrest or win us on the southern side! Turn not with disdain from yon cheerful-looking new building, the Union Workhouse, which enshrines, amid all this rising prosperity, " the short and simple annals of the poor." There are crabbed people who think it is " too fine a place for paupers," as I have more than once heard some of them say. Ah, my neighbours! Better, perchance, and worthier people than some outside have been brought more by misfortune than fault to end their days in a Union-house, however faulty some of those they have there to mate with may be! Lazarus was a beggar; and Dives, when he wanted water, became a beggar too. Listen, as I have sometimes done, to what such sensible guardians as Councillors Whitaker and Thompson could tell you, and learn to thank the whole Board for their humane pluck and care in providing such a retreat for those who require it.

And glancing up at yonder sweet rural home of the ancient Holden family amid its yet untainted southern pastures, as we proceed, let us next give a good look at both Brierfield, Nelson, and all around them, if only to compare them in another year or two with what may be developed *then*. And do not let us omit, as we pass still further on, a look at Marsden Hall, retreat for mental invalids, thankful that we live in an age, when mental infirmity can be as humanely and scientifically treated, as there is reason to believe it is, by Dr. Bennett, there. Its position is altogether one of the loveliest and liveliest, yet quietest, you could wish for such an institution.

Just one word more about Carr Hall, seat of Mr. Every-Clayton. Without at all monopolising, it and its domains do much to enrich the vale of Pendle-water flowing near its front, as it is seen from all the country round; and I trust no one will ever trespass, or otherwise abuse his privilege, in passing near on a forest, field or mountain pilgrimage.

And, but that I hope to take you on another occasion, I would ask you now to accompany me for a final view all around, including grand old Pendle, to the remains of the Roman encampment on Caster-Hill, or, as it is sometimes called, Tum-Hill, where, however, if all goes well, we may meet, perhaps some time next year, in another book of this kind—" Colne, Craven, and Scenes adjacent." *Au revoir !*

E. WRIGLEY AND SONS, PRINTERS, ROCHDALE.